M000251726

SRA

Reasoning and Writing

A Direct Instruction Program

Level B
Teacher's Guide

Siegfried Engelmann

Ann Brown Arbogast

Karen Lou Seitz Davis

Mc
Graw
Hill
Education

Cover Credits: (t)© Ingram Publishing/Alamy,
(b)Alan Sealls/WeatherVideoHD.TV

MHEonline.com

Copyright © McGraw-Hill Education

All rights reserved. No part of this publication may be
reproduced or distributed in any form or by any means, or
stored in a database or retrieval system, without the
prior written consent of McGraw-Hill Education,
including, but not limited to, network storage or
transmission, or broadcast for distance learning.

Permissions is granted to reproduce the material contained on
pages 96–99 on the condition that such material be reproduced
only for classroom use; be provided to students, teacher, or
families without charge; and be used solely in conjunction
with Reasoning and Writing.

Send all inquiries to:
McGraw-Hill Education
8787 Orion Place
Columbus, OH 43240

ISBN: 978-0-02-684766-7
MHID: 0-02-684766-3
Printed in the United States of America.

12 13 14 15 16 17 QVS 19 18 17 16 15

Contents

Program Summary

Facts about *Reasoning and Writing*, Level B

Children who are appropriately placed in Level B	Children who read and write on a beginning second-grade level
Format of lessons	Scripted presentations for all activities Program designed for presentation to entire class
Number of lessons	70 total (including 7 test lessons)
Scheduled time for Language periods	30–35 minutes per period for teacher-directed activities Additional 10–15 minutes for independent work
Weekly schedule	2, 3 or 5 periods per week. (Schedule depends on children's reading skills)
Teacher's material	Teacher's Guide Presentation Book Answer Key Book

Children's material	Program material:
	    Workbook 1, Lessons 1–35
	    Workbook 2, Lessons 36–70
	Additional materials:
	    crayon set that includes pink, purple and gray
	      (or a pencil for gray)
	    scissors
	    pencil
	    paste (Lesson 36)

In-program tests	Lessons 10, 20, 30, 40, 50, 60, 70
Remedies	See page 88, Test Remedies

Additional material	Writing Extension, Level B
	    Teacher's Presentation and
	      blackline masters for Extension
	      Lesson 1–60

Scope and Sequence for *Reasoning and Writing,* Level B

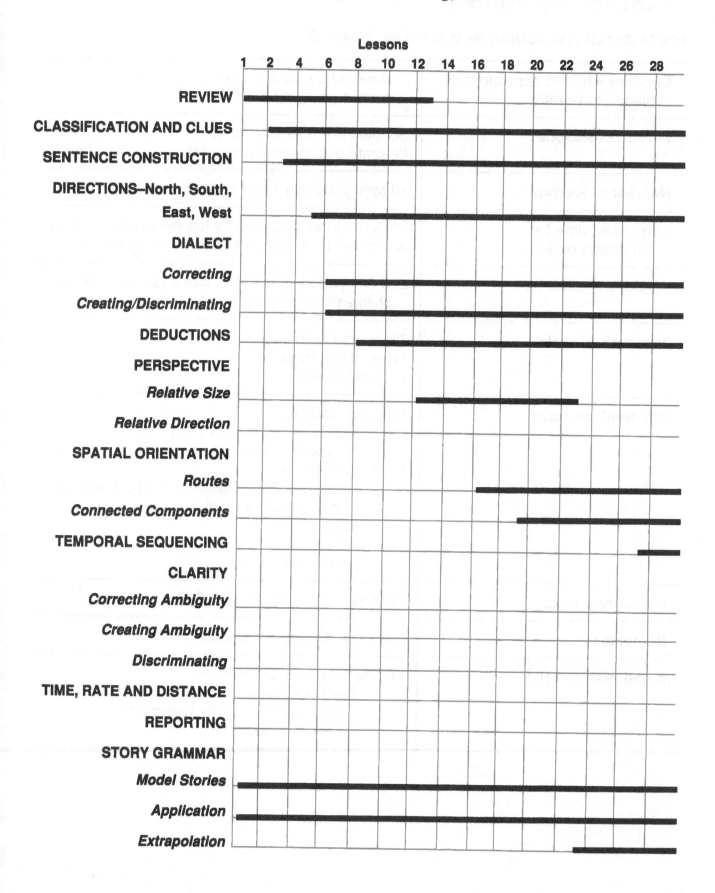

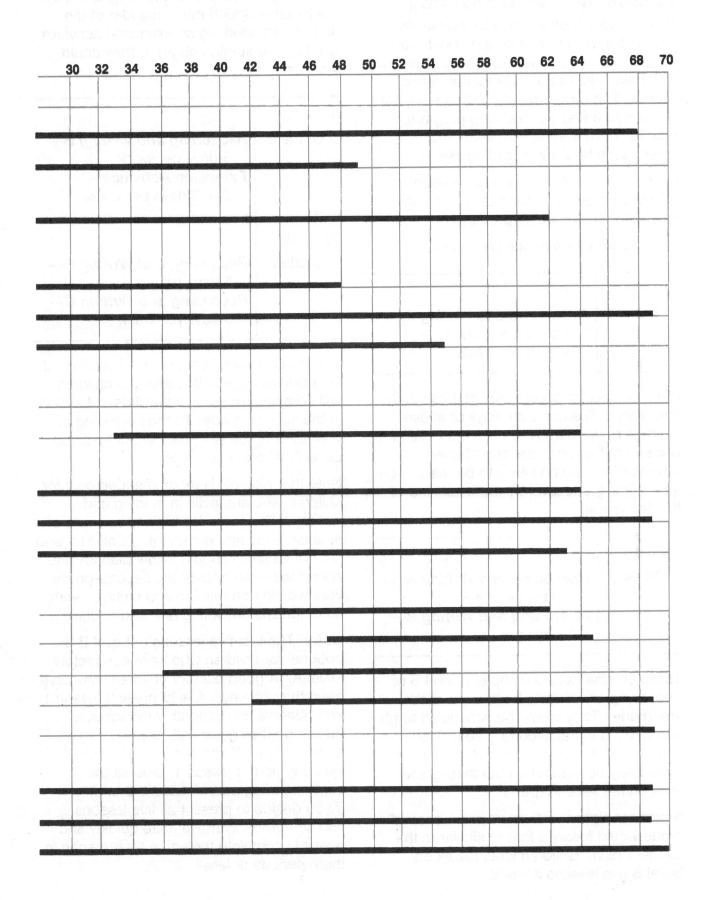

Placement and Scheduling

There is no placement test for *Reasoning and Writing B*. Level B is appropriate for children who have basic language skills and who have successfully completed a first-year reading program. (If children have not completed a first-year reading program, they will have trouble with items that presuppose beginning-reading skills.)

Reasoning and Writing B may be used in different ways, depending on the reading instruction that is being provided.

Here's a plan for average performers:

Plan 1	
Grade 2	*Reasoning and Writing B—* 2 days per week or 3 days per week

Here's a plan for accelerated children in the first grade. These are average or above-average performers who pass the Level A placement test and who are relatively advanced in reading (likely to be reading on a mid-first-grade level by the beginning of the first grade).

Plan 2	
Grade 1	*Reasoning and Writing A—* 5 days per week *Reasoning and Writing B—* 5 days per week

These children would complete Level B of *Reasoning and Writing* by the end of the first grade. They would be scheduled to go into Level C in the second grade. This schedule is reasonable for children who will most likely be reading on the third-grade level during second grade.

A plan for higher performers in the second grade would follow a format similar to the Grade-1 plan. Children would work on Level B five lessons a week.

Following completion of the program, they could either spend the remainder of the school year working on extension activities (writing and staging plays) or they could start Level C.

Plan 3A	
Grade 2	*Reasoning and Writing B—* 5 days per week **Extension Activities—** 2 or 3 days per week

Plan 3B	
Grade 2	*Reasoning and Writing B—* 5 days per week *Reasoning and Writing C—* 5 days per week

If plan 3B is used, it should be coordinated with the third grade because the children will complete possibly two-thirds of Level C in the second grade. At the beginning of their third-grade year, they should pick up Level C where they left off.

Note that plan 3B is recommended only for children who are facile in reading and writing. (They write legibly and at a rate of at least ten words per minute.) Children who are not as facile should follow plan 3A and spend the remainder of the second-grade year working on reading and writing—with an emphasis on writing rate and accuracy.

Note: The first five lessons of Level B are optional for children who have completed Level A. A good plan for children who have been through Level A is to present lesson 1 and observe how smoothly the various tasks go. If all goes well, skip to lesson 3 or 4. If children have difficulty with any part of lesson 1, present the corresponding part of lessons 2 and 3. If you decide to present all five lessons, you can probably move quite quickly and possibly complete the entire lesson span in three periods or less.

How the Program Is Different

Reasoning and Writing teaches higher-order thinking skills, the kind that are needed for later reading, writing and thinking. The program differs from traditional approaches to teaching these comprehension skills in the following ways:

FIELD-TESTED

Reasoning and Writing has been shaped through extensive field testing and revising based on problems children and teachers encountered. This work was completed before the program was published. The development philosophy of *Reasoning and Writing* is that if teachers or children have trouble with material presented, the program is at fault. Revisions are made to correct the problems.

ORGANIZATION

The organization of how skills are introduced, developed and reviewed is unique. In *Reasoning and Writing,* skills are organized in **tracks.** A track is an ongoing development of a particular topic. Within each lesson, work from 3 to 5 tracks is presented. The teaching presentations are designed so it is possible to present the entire lesson in 30 minutes (although some lessons may run longer and some shorter, and more time may be needed for lower performers).

From lesson to lesson, the work on new skills develops a small step at a time so that children are not overwhelmed with new information. Children receive enough practice both to master skills and become facile with them. Children, therefore, learn quickly about learning new concepts and realize that what they are learning has utility because they will use it.

In traditional programs, the curriculum is called a spiral, which means that children work exclusively on a particular topic for a few lessons. Then a new topic (often unrelated to the preceding topic) is presented. *Reasoning and Writing* does not follow this format for the following reasons:

a) During a period, it is not productive to work only on a single topic. If new information is being presented, it is very easy for children to become overwhelmed with the information. A more sensible procedure, and one that has been demonstrated to be superior in studies of learning and memory, is to distribute the practice so that, instead of working 30 minutes on a single topic, children work each day for possibly 7 minutes on each of four topics.

b) When full-period topics are presented, it becomes very difficult for the teacher to provide practice on the latest skills that have been taught. Unless the skills that have been taught are used and reviewed, children's performance will deteriorate, and the skills will have to be retaught when they again appear. A more sensible organization is to present work on skills continuously (not discontinuously), so that children work on a particular topic (such as deductions) for part of 20 or 30 lessons, not for 5 or 6 entire lessons at a time. In this context of continuous development of skills, review becomes automatic, and the need for reteaching is unlikely because children use the skills in almost every lesson.

c) When skills are not developed continuously, children must learn a lot of new concepts during a short period and are expected to become "automatic" in applying the new concepts and skills. For most children, adequate learning will not occur. A better method is to develop skills and concepts in small steps so that children are not required to learn as much new material at a time. In this way they receive a sufficient amount of practice to become facile or automatic in applying what they learn.

d) When skills are not developed continuously, children and teachers may develop very negative attitudes about mastery. Children often learn that they are not expected to "learn" the new material because it will go away in a few days. Teachers become frustrated because they often understand that children need much more practice, but they are unable to provide it and at the same time move through the program at a reasonable rate. Again, the continuous development of skills solves this problem because children learn very quickly that what is presented is used, in this lesson, the next lesson and in many subsequent lessons. When the practice is sufficient, children develop the mindset or expectation needed for learning mastery because the skill is something they will need in the immediate future.

e) When lessons are not clearly related to "periods" of time, the teacher has no precise way to gauge the performance of the children or to judge how long to spend on a particular "lesson." A more reasonable procedure is to organize material into lessons, each requiring so much time to teach. The teacher then knows that the lesson has the potential of teaching children within a class period of 30 minutes.

HIGHER-ORDER THINKING SKILLS

Reasoning and Writing **systematically teaches children to use higher-order thinking skills.** The program does not follow the current trends of merely exposing children to activities and assuming that they will learn something about reasoning or writing. The "exposure" approach is rejected in favor of systematic instruction for the following reasons:

a) Direct Instruction works best for teaching comprehension skills.

b) Later activities are more manageable if children have been taught the various component skills needed to engage meaningfully in the activities. When children are taught component skills, the teacher knows what the children have learned and can more easily correct mistakes. The correction does not involve extensive teaching during work on later activities, but merely reminds children of what they have already learned.

c) When all children are prepared for an elaborate activity, **all**—not some—can be expected to perform perfectly or near perfectly. The activity will not discriminate against lower performers (who often learn very little from an activity if they are simply exposed to it).

SKILLS THAT MATTER

All the skills taught in *Reasoning and Writing B* are important. These skills (a) are assumed by later work in reading, writing and content areas; (b) are typically not taught in any form; (c) can be taught uniformly to children who qualify for entering Level B.

The last feature is extremely important. You are probably familiar with traditional language series that introduce second graders to nouns, verbs, homonyms, homophones and various analyses of language. You are also probably familiar with writing programs that encourage children to write a great deal in the second grade.

The performance of children who go through these traditional programs provides ample information that the sequence of activities is not designed to teach—but merely to expose. Three years later, most of the children are not firm on the difference between a sentence and a non-sentence; most can't discriminate between a noun and a verb; and most show (through their writing and their punctuation) that they don't have the slightest idea of what constitutes a sentence. Level B does not present any grammatical analysis, formal sentence analysis or work on sophisticated topics like homophones.

Rather, the topics and skills presented in Level B are those that relate to what children can do and what they will be reasonably required to do in the following grades. The activities in Level B focus on laying a solid conceptual foundation for later writing and analysis of language.

PREPARATION FOR READING, WRITING AND CONTENT AREAS

The higher-order thinking skills presented in *Reasoning and Writing B* are designed to prepare children for later work in reading, writing and reasoning in content areas.

a) **Story Grammar.** When children read, they are expected to get a sense of the story so they can anticipate what will happen and can relate events that occur to what they know about the characters or the situations presented. To prepare students for this type of understanding, Level B expands on what children know about story grammar.

b) **Sequencing and Spatial Orientation.** Children are expected to work with a static illustration or diagram and to interpret it as an event that is related to events that preceded it and events that follow. In Level B, children do a lot of work with temporal sequencing of events by interpreting pictures and diagrams.

c) **Classification.** The major thrust of classification in Level B is to use information to eliminate possibilities. Children play a lot of clue games where they use information provided through clues to identify the mystery character or the mystery sequence. Children also do manipulations in which they make classes larger or smaller by manipulating subclasses that are within the larger class.

d) **Following Instructions and Writing Instructions.** Activities in Level B are designed so that children follow precise directions. Many of the activities involve maps. Children follow directions that involve distance and direction: "Go four blocks north; turn to the west and go three blocks." Children also make up such directions to get to specified objects.

e) **Constructing Deductions and Drawing Conclusions.** Later work in math, science, social studies and reading assumes an understanding of deductions and how to draw a conclusion from properly presented facts. Level B presents children with a model that makes drawing conclusions easy. The model also allows children to identify deductions that are formally incorrect.

f) **Clarity.** Children work with pronoun clarity. "The bugs were in the bushes. They were red." The passage could have two meanings. The bugs could be red or the bushes could be red. Level B presents many clarity activities in which children learn to identify the "unclear" word in passages like the one above. Children also learn to translate the possible meanings into concrete images. For example, they color pictures to show the two meanings for the passage above. (One picture has bugs that are red; the other has bushes that are red.)

g) **Time, Rate and Distance.** Level B sharpens what children already know about these phenomena and introduces concepts and applications that prepare children for more precise work in math, science and general understanding. Children work with illustrations of different types of racetracks, where they act out races. Some racetracks show where the two racers are after 1 . . . 2 . . . 3 . . . seconds. Children answer comprehension questions about the amount of time it takes a racer to reach the finish line and how fast the racer runs. (The longer it takes, the slower the racer is.) On later racetracks, units of distance (feet, inches, miles) are introduced. Children make up rules that tell how much distance each racer covers in a second (or a minute).

h) Perspectives. Much of what children do in Level B prompts different perspectives. The Level B stories give children information about motives that permit them to predict what will happen to familiar characters. The work with maps and diagrams prompts children to view static diagrams as sources of information about events that are linked to each other. Activities involving relative size and relative direction give children practice at viewing things from different perspectives.

i) Writing. In Level B, children work largely with sentences. Many of the sentences they write are prompted by illustrations. The format children follow for composing sentences is to name and then tell more. (Name the character; tell the main thing the character did.) This "sentence format" prepares children for sentence analysis (which starts in Level C with subject-predicate). Children create simple stories that involve thematically related sentences. Later activities in the program introduce children to expressing inferences. Two pictures show things that happened. Between the pictures is a blank picture. Children learn to compare the details of the pictures so they can write about the events that must have occurred in the blank picture. Finally, children learn to discriminate between sentences that report on what a picture shows and sentences that do not report. This skill is also important for later writing.

Stories

The central focus of each lesson is the story. The story typically comes at the end of the lesson. For the children, it's the payoff—the dessert. It is also the vehicle that both integrates what children learn and teaches them about the structure of stories. While it teaches "story grammar," the teaching focus is like that of the other activities in Level B—on construction.

Children learn about stories in such a way that they can construct stories according to the constraints of different story grammars.

Part of each lesson presents a story or an activity that derives from one of the stories. All stories in Level B are designed to teach and expand on the concepts that are being taught to the children. Also, each major story has a unique story grammar that permits children to predict what will happen when a familiar character is engaged in a new adventure and permits them to create new stories based on the story grammar. Here's a list of the stories and the lesson in which each story is first presented. The stories in the first five lessons are stories that also appeared in Level A.

Lesson	Story
1	Paul Paints Plums
2	The Bragging Rats Race
3	Sweetie and the Birdbath
4	Clarabelle and the Bluebirds
5	Roger and the Headstand
6	Bleep Says Some Strange Things, Part 1
8	Paul Paints Pansies
11	The Mouse and the Toadstool
12	Bleep Says Some Strange Things, Part 2
15	Goober
16	Owen and the Little People, Part 1
17	Owen and the Little People, Part 2
18	Owen and the Little People, Part 3
19	Owen and the Little People, Part 4
22	Owen and the Little People, Part 5
23	Owen and the Little People, Part 6
25	The Bragging Rat Wants to Be a Detective
29	Dot and Dud, Part 1
32	Dot and Dud, Part 2
33	Dot and Dud, Part 3
34	Zelda the Artist, Part 1
35	Zelda the Artist, Part 2
36	Zelda the Artist, Part 3
38	The Case of the Missing Corn, Part 1
39	The Case of the Missing Corn, Part 2

The stories at the beginning of Level B (Paul, Sweetie, Clarabelle) were introduced in Level A. Here are summaries of the unique story grammars introduced in Level B.

BLEEP AND MOLLY

Bleep is a robot who talks and reasons. He sometimes removes the top of his head and fiddles with the screws that control the way he talks. He first adjusts two screws, causing him to be unable to say the short **e** sound. Instead, he says the short **u** sound. When trying to say "I will rest now," he says, "I will rust now."

In a later story, his creator, Molly, discovers that he is unable to say **s-l** combinations. He drops the **l** sound. Instead of saying "The stairs are slick," he says, "The stairs are sick."

In still another episode, Bleep adjusts his screws so that he talks like someone with a clothespin on his nose. He is unable to say the sounds for **m** and **n.** Instead of "win," he says, "wid." Instead of saying "mud," he says, "bud."

In a final episode, Bleep adjusts his speech so that he can't say the short **a** sound. Instead of saying "I am mad," he says, "I um mud."

The activities associated with Bleep stories capitalize on transforming dialect or correcting dialect. These activities both reinforce what children are learning about sounds and sound combinations and, at the same time, permit the children to play with codes that transform many utterances into "Bleep-talk."

GOOBER

Goober is a farmer whose story grammar is associated with sounds and smells. The sounds come from Goober's violin, which he plays beautifully. The smells come from Goober's pigs. Goober's pigs smell so bad that when people are around them, they hold their nose. Goober's problems end when a little girl from a nearby town brings him soap for pigs. Goober bathes his pigs and they no longer smell bad. Then the people can enjoy his beautiful violin music without being distracted.

Goober's adventures lead naturally to work with maps and directions. When the wind blows over his farm from west to east, his smell drifts to the town to the east of his farm. When the wind blows from east to west, the town to the west suffers. Goober's story grammar also leads to activities involving transformed speech and sound transformations. Children correct the speech of people who are holding their nose and saying things like "By dabe is Barry." (My name is Mary.)

OWEN, FIZZ AND LIZ

Owen and the Little People is a story about a giant (Owen) on one island and two very tiny characters (Fizz and Liz) on another identical island. Fizz and Liz are only about an inch tall. Owen has never seen Fizz and Liz, so he doesn't know how little they are. He communicates with them by sending notes in a bottle. He tries to describe his island. He tells how big things are by comparing the things to himself. On the other hand, Fizz and Liz don't know how big Owen is. They write answers by telling how different things are on their island. On Owen's island, there are very small bears. On the island of the little people, a bear's claw is bigger than a full-grown person.

Owen and his family decide to visit the island of Fizz and Liz. When they reach the island, they think that they must have made a mistake by returning to their own island. Finally, Owen locates Fizz and Liz and helps the little people with the construction of their community center.

The series about Owen and the little people presents many examples of perspective and relative size. It serves as a point of departure for measuring different things with "non-standard" units. For some workbook exercises, children use a "stack" of Fizzes and Lizzes to measure the height of objects. The height is expressed as "three times as tall as we are" or "five times as tall as we are." The series also reinforces concepts such as directions (north, south, east, west) and "continuous movement" (complicated routes that objects follow).

SHERLOCK AND BERTHA

Sherlock is one of the bragging rats from Level A. He decides to become a detective. One of his major problems is that he doesn't understand formal deductions or how to use clues to eliminate possibilities. Sherlock enlists the help of a beetle named Bertha to work with him. Bertha's role is to be that of a tracker. (She has a very good nose.) Although she is shy and initially reluctant to comment on Sherlock's plans, she has a good understanding of deductions and clues. She assists Sherlock first in the adventure of the missing corn. The rat pack's corn is stored in a barn and the supply is dwindling. Someone is stealing it. Sherlock makes this faulty deduction about the corn thief: The corn thief went into the barn; the red hen went into the barn; so the red hen is the corn thief. Sherlock tells the rat pack how he discovered the corn thief, and the rats start to use Sherlock's deduction to accuse each other. "**You** went into the barn, too. So you must have stolen the corn."

Bertha manages to straighten things out and later solves the crime. In another adventure, she and Sherlock use inferences to discover what happened to the squash that was being saved for the rat pack's annual fall feast.

The episodes with Bertha and Sherlock reinforce what children learn about deductions and clues. Some of the activities that accompany the stories present formally incorrect deductions, and the children have to identify their flaws. The series also lends itself to plays and to the creation of parallel adventures.

DOT AND DUD

Another major series of stories is about two St. Bernards, Dot and Dud. They are siblings who work as rescue dogs in the mountains. Dot is diligent; Dud has the potential to be a great tracker, but he is lazy and playful. In their first episode, Dud gets separated from the ranger and the other dogs on a climb to find a stranded mountain climber. Dud becomes disoriented, goes in the wrong direction and ends up in the kitchen of a ski lodge miles to the south of the stranded climber. In the meantime, Dot finds the climber but is separated from the rescue party. Near nightfall, the party abandons the search and returns to the ranger station for the night. Dud finds out that Dot is not with the other dogs. With determination, he tracks her that evening. The others follow him up the mountain, where they reach Dot and the stranded climber.

The Dot and Dud episodes reinforce what children have learned about "work dogs" (as part of classification exercises), about directions, maps, continuous movement, and how events may be correlated (the higher you go up the mountain, the colder the air gets).

ZELDA AND MRS. HUDSON

The Zelda and Mrs. Hudson stories teach children very sophisticated skills about clarity of expression. Zelda is a talented artist who is far better at illustrating than she is at interpreting unclear directions. Mrs. Hudson is the writer of a very boring book about her experiences. The book contains many unclear parts. Zelda agrees to do illustrations for Mrs. Hudson's book, and the results are humorous to the reader, but devastating to Mrs. Hudson.

To illustrate this part of the book—"My brother and my sister had pet pigs. They just loved to roll around in the mud."—Zelda draws a picture of the brother and sister rolling in the mud.

To illustrate this part of the book—"We always kept a glass on top of the refrigerator. We kept it full of water."— Zelda, with some difficulty, illustrates the refrigerator full of water.

Although Mrs. Hudson hates Zelda's illustrations, the book is a smash because of them.

The Zelda episodes serve as a point of departure for work on clarity. Typically, second graders do not understand unclear pronoun references. They quickly learn about clarity within the humorous context of Zelda's illustrations. The work on pronoun references (clarity) is expanded and becomes a major focus of Level B. Worksheet exercises require children to edit parts of Mrs. Hudson's story so the parts do not contain unclear pronouns, to draw illustrations for parts that have unclear pronouns and to construct passages that have unclear pronouns. This work, and the understanding that underlies it, is very important for writing and for understanding exercises in later levels of *Reasoning and Writing*.

In addition to alerting children to read a passage critically for possible ambiguity, the Zelda stories prompt children to imagine what the passage would say if the unintentional meaning were selected. Children indicate how Zelda would illustrate unclear passages.

DOOLY THE DUCK

The sequence about Dooly the Duck focuses on a different spectrum of skills— following instructions, including those that involve relative direction (east of something but west of something else). Dooly is a Mallard duck who molts late one summer and cannot go with the other Mallards down the flyway to Mexico for the winter. He must remain in Minnesota while his feathers grow in. Then he will fly down to Mexico by himself.

Before the others leave, the head of the flock gives him directions about the first safe landing spot along the flyway. The landing place is between a hill and a walnut-shaped lake in Nebraska. The safe spot is "south of the hill and north of the lake." Dooly has a lot of trouble following these directions. After landing in the wrong place, he finally lands in the safe spot, where a crow teaches him more about following instructions that involve relative directions. Dooly learns fast and makes the trip to Mexico in record time. Later, he becomes the leader of the flock and successfully guides the flock on their annual migrations.

The Dooly stories reinforce what children have learned about relative direction and maps. The stories introduce the "flyway" that goes south from Minnesota to Mexico. Children learn the name of some states and become familiar with the map of North America—knowledge that will serve them well in later grades.

DESSERA

The story about Dessera is the last sequence in Level B. Dessera is Queen of Garbo. She is young and headstrong. She visits the Rocky Mountains, where she plans to ski and climb mountains. Despite warnings from the ranger, she takes two of her greyhounds with her on a climb. Soon, the greyhounds get separated from the climbers. Dessera decides to look for them by herself and slides down a slope to a precarious ledge. The others in her party return to the ranger station to form a rescue team. Dot and Dud are among the dogs in this team. After they lead the way to Dessera, they find the exhausted greyhounds huddling in a cave. Dud challenges them by asserting that they are sissies and couldn't catch him in a race down the mountain. The ploy works, and the greyhounds chase Dud to safety.

The Dessera stories lead to further work with the map of North America. They also introduce rules about "correlated events." (The higher you go in the mountains, the colder it gets. The higher you go in the mountains, the harder it is to breathe . . . .) For some workbook activities, children indicate on a diagram of a mountain which places are colder, which places have less air, and so forth.

ZENA AND ZOLA

Zena and Zola are Zelda's sisters. Together they write reports that are clear. Separately, they write accounts that are vague. Zola writes elaborate subjects but vague predicates. For Zena, the subjects are vague, but the predicates are detailed.

SUMMARY

In summary, the stories in Level B meet the major criterion of being enjoyable. Children find them entertaining. The stories also serve as melting pots to integrate the various skills that are taught in the program and to introduce extensions and new skills. The stories serve very important instructional purposes. They acquaint children with an extended variety of story grammars and provide opportunities for them to engage in productive creative endeavors.

The stories are the last part of the lessons. They serve as a motivator for the other lesson activities. Although children generally treat them as dessert, the stories are very powerful vehicles for teaching skills that are both sophisticated and useful.

Teaching the Program

Level B is designed to be presented to the entire class. You should generally be able to teach one lesson during a 30–35 minute period. Children's independent work requires another 10–15 minutes. The independent work can be scheduled at another time during the day.

Organization

Arrange seating so you can receive very quick information on high performers and low performers. A good plan is to organize the children something like this:

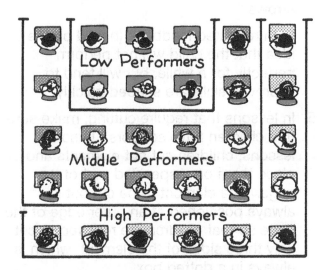

The lowest performers are closest to the front of the classroom. Middle performers are arranged around the lowest performers. Highest performers are arranged around the periphery. With this arrangement, you can position yourself so that, by taking a few steps during the time that children are working problems, you can sample low, average and high performers.

While different variations of this arrangement are possible, be careful not to seat low performers far from the front-center of the room. The highest performers, understandably, can be farthest from the center because they attend better, learn faster, and need less observation and feedback.

For some activities, children will work in groups or teams. The size of the groups varies. When assigning groups, make sure that each group has a range of children. (Don't put all the higher performers in one group.)

Teaching

When you teach the program, a basic rule is that you shouldn't present from the front of the room unless you're showing something on the board.

For most of the activities, you direct children to work specified tasks. For these activities, you should present from somewhere in the middle of the room (in no set place); and as children work the task, you should move around and quickly observe a good sample of children. Although you won't be able to observe every child working every task, you can observe at least half a dozen children in possibly 15 seconds.

Rehearse the lesson before presenting it to the class. Don't simply read the text—act it out.

Watch your wording. If you rehearse each of the early lessons before presenting it, you'll soon learn how to present efficiently from the script. In later lessons, you should scan the list of skills at the beginning of each lesson. New skills are in boldface type. If a new skill is introduced in a lesson, rehearse it. Most activities in the lesson will not be new, but will be a variation of what you've presented earlier, so you may not need to rehearse these activities.

Managing Activities

The emphasis of Level B is on constructing outcomes. Children make arrows, color things according to rules, measure, cut, and arrange. In most lessons, children use pencil and crayons. In some lessons, children also use scissors. Children often lack facility in working quickly and efficiently with this material.

Here are general management procedures for shaping their behavior.

1. Make sure that each child has the material needed for the lesson. One plan is to announce at the beginning of the lesson that it's time for the language lesson. Introduce the rule that you'll count to ten. All children who have their pencil and crayons on their desk and in place by the time you finish counting receive a good-work point (or sticker).

2. Establish the rule that children are not to play with their crayons or pencil until you tell them to use them. "Remember, don't play with your material." The simplest way to shape their behavior is to praise children who are working "big." "Wow, we have a lot of big people in this room. Everybody has their pencil and crayons in place and nobody is playing with them. Nice job." If playing with material becomes a problem, award bonus points (or stickers) for not playing with the material.

3. When pencils or crayons are used for activities that precede the story, establish rules for what children are to do with their material when they complete the activity. "Remember, when you're finished, crayons back in the box. Pencils back in place." Again, praise children who follow these rules.

   "I can tell a lot of people are already finished because I see a lot of desks with the material in its place. Good work."

After the structured lesson has been completed, children color the story picture and possibly other parts of the worksheet. This activity does not have to be scheduled as part of the lesson, but can be presented during "seat work" time.

4. Demonstrate procedures that require mechanical skills. Some children often have trouble writing or drawing arrows quickly. The simplest way to shape this behavior is to tell the child: "You want to see somebody who knows how to do a super job? Watch me." Quickly complete the job. "See if you can do that." Observe the child later and give feedback on improvements. "You're doing a lot better—those are good arrows."

   With repeated feedback (based on the idea that the child will not perform perfectly for a while, but will tend to improve), skills are shaped quickly.

5. In lessons that require cutting, make sure that children have scissors. In some lessons, children cut out elements and place them on a specified part of the page. The element to be cut out is always positioned at an outer edge of the page so that children are required to cut only three sides of the element, which is always in a dotted box.

6. Many lessons require children to "draw" elements or write letters or words in the picture. The simplest way to shape this type of activity is to post children's material where all can see it. A good plan is to post samples of good work.

   All children have their best work posted. The material remains on display for one week. When children do a particularly good job on a part, reward them by posting that worksheet. "That's a super job of coloring that picture and writing all the words. We're going to put this worksheet on display."

7. Present extension activities that give children an opportunity to use what they've learned in Level B.

The suggestions provided at the end of lesson 70 are for children to do at least four projects that are extensions of their work in Level B. These are:

A story

A play

A book

A map

All these projects are conducted in small groups. The book that children write is an illustrated book that may contain one or more illustrated stories written by each of the cooperating authors of the book.

Typically, a three-lesson-per-week schedule will allow children to complete lesson 70 before the end of March. The remainder of the school year provides time for children to engage in one play, write one story, work on one complicated map, and help construct a book.

If children are not writing at least ten words per minute at the end of Level B, devote at least part of the remaining periods to work on writing. Write short passages on the board and have the children copy them. If children are not writing at least ten words per minute when they enter Level C, they will have trouble with the Level C writing activities.

Using the Teacher Presentation Scripts

The script for each lesson indicates precisely how to present each structured activity. The script shows what you say, what you do and what the children's responses should be.

What you say appears in blue type:
You say this.

What you do appears in parentheses:
(You do this.)

The responses of the children are in italics:
Children say this.

Follow the specified wording in the script. While wording variations from the specified script are not always dangerous, you will be assured of communicating clearly with the children if you follow the script exactly. The reason is that the wording is controlled, and the tasks are arranged so they provide succinct wording and focus clearly on important aspects of what the children are to do. Although you may at first feel uncomfortable "reading" from a script (and you may feel that the children will not pay attention), follow the scripts very closely; try to present them as if you were saying something important to the children. If you do, you'll find after awhile that working from a script is not difficult and that children indeed respond well to what you say.

A sample script appears on the next page.

3. Everybody, touch picture 1. ✔
   Who's in that picture? (Signal.) *Roger.*
• What did Roger do in this picture?
   (Call on a child. Idea: *Sat on a hat.*)
• Here's the sentence that tells what Roger did:
   Roger sat on a hat.

1 ➤ **How you secure group responses**

4. Everybody, say that sentence. (Signal.)
   Roger sat on a hat.
   (Repeat step 4 until firm.)
5. For each space on the arrow, you'll write the words
   that are in one of the boxes below the arrow:
6. Touch the first space on the arrow for picture 1. ✔
   What will you write in that space? (Signal.) *Roger*
• Touch the middle space. ✔
   What will you write in that space? (Signal.) *Sat on.*
• Touch the last space? ✔
   What will you write in that space? *A hat.*
   (Repeat step 6 until firm.)

3 **What you firm**

7. Your turn: Write sentence 1. Remember to spell the
   words correctly. Start with a capital letter and end
   with a period. Rasie your hand when you're
   finished. (Observe children and give feedback.)

2 ➤ **What you write**

• (Write on the board:)

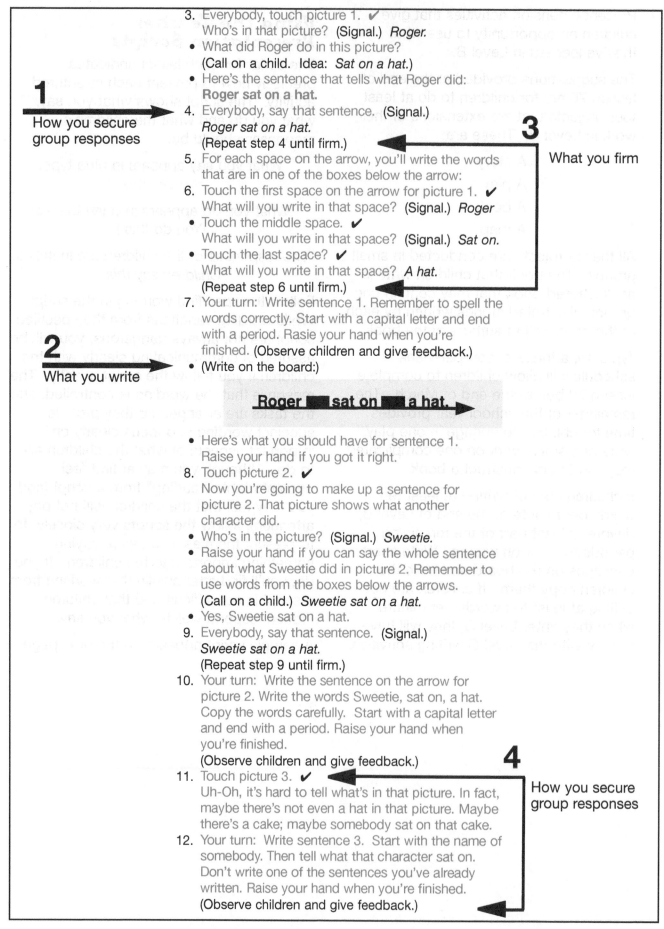

Roger ▮ sat on ▮ a hat. ➤

• Here's what you should have for sentence 1.
   Raise your hand if you got it right.
8. Touch picture 2. ✔
   Now you're going to make up a sentence for
   picture 2. That picture shows what another
   character did.
• Who's in the picture? (Signal.) *Sweetie.*
• Raise your hand if you can say the whole sentence
   about what Sweetie did in picture 2. Remember to
   use words from the boxes below the arrows.
   (Call on a child.) *Sweetie sat on a hat.*
• Yes, Sweetie sat on a hat.
9. Everybody, say that sentence. (Signal.)
   Sweetie sat on a hat.
   (Repeat step 9 until firm.)
10. Your turn: Write the sentence on the arrow for
    picture 2. Write the words Sweetie, sat on, a hat.
    Copy the words carefully. Start with a capital letter
    and end with a period. Raise your hand when
    you're finished.
    (Observe children and give feedback.)
11. Touch picture 3. ✔
    Uh-Oh, it's hard to tell what's in that picture. In fact,
    maybe there's not even a hat in that picture. Maybe
    there's a cake; maybe somebody sat on that cake.

4 **How you secure group responses**

12. Your turn: Write sentence 3. Start with the name of
    somebody. Then tell what that character sat on.
    Don't write one of the sentences you've already
    written. Raise your hand when you're finished.
    (Observe children and give feedback.)

The arrows show the four different things you'll do that are not spelled out in the script.

- You'll make sure that group responses involve all the children.
- For some exercises, you'll write things on the board.
- You'll also "firm" critical parts of the exercises.
- And you'll use information based on what the children are doing to judge whether you'll proceed quickly or wait a few more seconds before moving on with the presentation.

ARROW 1: GROUP RESPONSES

Some tasks call for an individual child to respond. Some tasks call for group responses. If children respond in unison, you receive good information about whether "most" of the children are performing correctly. The simplest way to signal children to respond together is to adopt a timing practice—just like the timing in a musical piece.

Step 4 presents a task that children respond to in unison:

Everybody, say that sentence. (Signal.)
Roger sat on a hat.

You can signal when children are to respond by nodding, clapping one time, snapping your fingers or tapping your foot. After initially establishing the timing for signals, you can signal through voice inflection only.

Children will not be able to respond together at the appropriate rate unless you follow these rules:

a) Talk first. Pause a standard length of time (possibly 1 second); then signal. Children are to respond on your signal—not after it or before it.

b) Model responses that are paced reasonably. Don't permit children to produce slow, drony responses. These are dangerous because they rob you of the information that can be derived from appropriate group responses. When children respond in a drony way, many of them are copying responses of others. If children are required to respond at a reasonable speaking rate, all children must initiate responses; therefore, it's relatively easy to determine which children are not responding and which are saying the wrong thing.

Also, don't permit children to respond at a very fast rate or to "jump" your signal.

To correct mistakes, show children exactly what you want them to do:

- I'm good at saying it the right way. My turn to say that sentence. **Roger sat on a hat.** Wasn't that great? Let's see who can do it just that way.
  Everybody, say that sentence. (Signal.)
  Roger sat on a hat.
  Good saying it the right way.

(**Note:** Do **not** respond with the children unless you are trying to work with them on a difficult response. You present only what's in blue. You do not say the answers with the children, and you should not move your lips or give other spurious clues about what the answer is.)

Think of unison responses this way: If you use them correctly, they provide you with much diagnostic information. They suggest whether you should repeat a task (because the response was weak). They permit you to get information about which children may need more help. They are therefore important early in the program. After children have learned the game, the children will be able to respond on cue with no signal. That will happen, however, only if you always keep a constant time interval between the completion of what you say and your signal.

ARROW 2: BOARD WORK

What you write is indicated in the display boxes of the script. In the sample exercise, you make an arrow with boxes and words.

Scanning the display boxes in the script shows both what you'll write and how you'll change displays.

ARROW 3: FIRMING

When children make mistakes, you correct them. A correction may occur during any part of the teacher presentation that calls for children to respond. Here are the rules for corrections:

- You correct a mistake as soon as you hear it.
- A mistake on oral responses is saying the wrong thing or not responding.

In step 4, children may not say anything or may not correctly say "Roger sat on a hat." You correct as soon as you hear the mistake. You do not wait until children finish responding before correcting.

To correct, say the correct response and then repeat the task they missed.

> Some children: *Roger was . . .*
> Teacher: Roger sat on a hat.
> Your turn: Say that sentence.

Sometimes, one step in the exercise involves a series of oral tasks. In step 6, children produce these responses:

6. Touch the first space on the arrow for picture 1. ✔
   What will you write in that space?
   (Signal.) *Roger.*
- Touch the middle space. ✔
   What will you write in that space?
   (Signal.) *Sat on.*
- Touch the last space. ✔
   What will you write in that space?
   (Signal.) *A hat.*
   (Repeat step 6 until firm.)

After correcting any mistakes **within** this series of tasks, you would return to the beginning of step 6 and present the entire step.

The note **(Repeat step ____ until firm)** occurs when children must correctly produce a series of responses. When you "repeat until firm," you follow these steps:

1) Correct the mistake. (Tell the response and repeat the **task** that was missed.)
2) Return to the beginning of the specified step and present the entire step.

"Repeating until firm" provides information you need about the children. When the children made the mistake, you told the answer. Did they remember the answer? Would they now be able to perform the step correctly? The repeat-until-firm procedure provides you with answers to these questions. You present the context in which the mistake occurred and the children can show you through their responses whether or not the correction worked, whether or not they are **firm.**

The repeat-until-firm direction appears only on the most critical parts of new-teaching exercises. It usually focuses on knowledge that is very important for the work the children are to do. If you didn't firm the children in step 6 of the exercise, in step 7 you would find some children writing words in the wrong place or not doing anything. You would have to correct each child individually, telling each what to do. By repeating until firm, you potentially save time because you have made sure that children are firm in their understanding of where the words go.

As a general procedure, follow the repeat-until-firm directions. However, if you're quite sure that the mistake was a "glitch" and does not mean that the children lack understanding, don't follow the repeat-until-firm direction.

The specified responses for some tasks are not what some children might say. Expect variability in some group responses. Accept any reasonable wording.

If you want to hold children to the wording that is in the script (which is not necessary for tasks that can be reasonably answered in other ways), say something like, "That's right." Then say the response you want. "Everybody, say it that way."

As a rule, if more than one answer is possible for the task you presented and you know that the children's answers are reasonable, don't bother with a correction. Just move on to the next part of the teacher script.

ARROW 4: PACING YOUR PRESENTATION

You should pace your verbal presentation at a normal speaking rate—as if you were telling somebody something important.

(**Note:** The presentation works much better and the inflections are far more appropriate if you pretend that you're talking to an **adult,** not a young child. Make your message sound important.)

The most typical mistake teachers make is going too slowly or talking as if to preschoolers.

The arrows for number 4 show two ways to pace your presentation for activities in which children write or draw or touch or find parts of their workbook page. The first is a note to **(Observe children and give feedback).** The second is a ✔ mark. That's a note to check what the children are doing.

A ✔ requires only a second or two. If you are positioned close to several "average performing" students, check whether they are performing. If they are, proceed with the presentation.

The **(Observe children and give feedback)** direction implies a more elaborate response. You sample more children and you give feedback, not only to individual children, but to the group. Here are the basic rules for what to do and not do when you observe and give feedback.

1) Make sure that you are not at the front of the class when you present the directions for tasks that involve observing children's performance. When you direct children to write the sentence about Sweetie, move to a place where you can quickly sample the performance of low, middle, and high performers.

2) As soon as children start to work, start observing. As you observe, make comments to the whole class. Focus these comments on children who are (a) following directions, (b) working quickly, (c) working accurately. "Wow, a couple of children are almost finished. I haven't seen one mistake so far."

3) When children raise their hand to indicate that they are finished, acknowledge them. (When you acknowledge that they are finished, they are to put their hand down.)

4) If you observe mistakes, do **not** provide a great deal of individual help. Point out any mistakes, but do not do the work for the children. Point to the problem and say, "I think you made a mistake here. Look at the word 'Sweetie' in the box and see how it is spelled."

If children are not following instructions that you gave, tell them, "You're supposed to write the whole sentence. Listen very carefully to my instructions."

5) Do **not** wait for the slowest children to complete the activities before presenting the work check, during which children correct their work and fix up any mistakes. A good rule early in the program is to allow a **reasonable amount of time.** You can usually use the middle performers as a gauge for what is reasonable. As you observe that they are completing their work, announce, "Okay, you have about ten seconds more to finish up." At the end of that time, continue in the exercise.

6) Continue to circulate among the children and make sure that they fix up any mistakes you identify.

7) If you observe a serious problem that is not unique to only the lowest performers, tell the class, "Stop. We seem to have a serious problem." Repeat the part of the exercise that gives them information about what they are to do.

   (*Note:* Do not provide "new teaching." Simply repeat the part of the exercise that gives them the information they need and reassign the work. "Let's see who can get it this time. . . .")

8) While children do their independent work (coloring their pictures), you may want to go over any parts of the lesson with the children who had trouble. At this time, you can show them what they did wrong. Keep your explanations simple. The more you talk, the more you'll probably confuse them. If there are serious problems, repeat the exercise that presented difficulties for the lower performers.

SUMMARY

The four arrows indicate how you'll interact with the children, Where you say something that requires them to respond, they may make a mistake. You should anticipate that possibility and be ready to correct. Some steps in an exercise are more critical than others. If children are to do things that are either mechanically difficult or conceptually difficult, you want to "pre-correct" as many mistakes as possible. These parts of the format are usually flagged with a note to **(Repeat until firm).** You want to make sure that the children are keeping up with your presentation, that they are attending to what you say. The parts of the exercise with ✔ marks and the **(Observe and give feedback)** are your key for judging whether the children are attending and performing.

You want to give them feedback. You let them know when they are performing well in following your directions and when they are making mistakes. For some types of feedback, you'll write on the board. You'll also write on the board to show them how things work.

When you practice exercises in the program, look at the places where you interact with the children. Those are places where mistakes may occur and where you may have to respond to what the children are doing.

Shaping Children's Performance

The directions for presenting the teacher script provide you with information about how to hold the children's attention and how to pace your presentation so you're responsive to them and they are following your directions. Some of the lower performers may require "shaping" that goes beyond the details provided by the lesson script. Ideally, you should shape these children so they can keep up with the rest of the class when you present **at a reasonable pace.** If you key your presentation to the lower performers, nobody benefits. You actually punish the higher and middle performers and make the lessons boring for most of the children. Here are some general shaping suggestions that will help you accommodate all the children except those who do not have the skills necessary to begin Level B.

If children take a great deal of time writing, coloring, or drawing elements, use a timer to shape their performance. First, observe average performers and see how long it takes them to complete the tasks that are time consuming. Use that information for establishing a baseline. If average performers take 30 seconds to write a sentence, set the criterion for 30 seconds.

Tell children, "I'm setting the timer for 30 seconds. So you'll have to work pretty fast. But work carefully. Raise your hand when you're finished."

As children raise their hand before the timer goes off, quickly check their work and make announcements, such as, "Wow, a lot of people are working fast and carefully."

When the timer goes off, say, "Everybody who finished, raise your hand. . . . Next time, we'll see if we have even more children who can finish before the timer goes off." Either allow the children who didn't finish a little more time, or present the next activity to the class with the understanding that you'll work later with the children who didn't finish.

Although this procedure may seem harsh, it will very quickly shape the performance of children who are physically capable of performing.

When performance improves and virtually all children are completing the task on time, change the criterion. "I'm not going to set the timer for 30 seconds. I'm going to make it harder and set it for 25. That's going to be really tough. Let's see who can do it."

Continue to change the criterion as children improve until they are performing at an acceptable rate.

If you follow these pacing procedures, your children will work faster and more accurately. They will also become facile at following your directions.

If you don't follow these rules, you may think that you are **helping** children, but you will actually be reinforcing them for behaviors that you are trying to change. If you wait far beyond a reasonable time period before presenting the work check, you punish the higher performers and the others who worked quickly and accurately. Soon, they will learn that there is no "payoff" for doing well—no praise, no recognition—but instead a long wait while you give attention to lower performers.

If you don't make announcements about children who are doing well and working quickly, the class will not understand what's expected. Children will probably not improve much.

If you provide extensive individual help on independent work, you will actually reinforce children for not listening to your directions, for being dependent on your help. Furthermore, this dependency becomes contagious. If you provide extensive individual "guidance," it doesn't take other children in the class long to discover that they don't have to listen to your directions, that they can raise their hand and receive help and that children who have the most serious problems receive the most teacher attention. These expectations are the opposite of the ones you want to induce. You want children to be self-reliant and to have a **reason** for learning and remembering what you say when you instruct them. The simplest reason is that they will use what they have just been shown and that those who remember will receive reinforcement.

If you provide wordy explanations and extensive reteaching to correct any problems you observe, you run the risk of further confusing the children. Their problem is that they didn't attend to or couldn't perform on some detail that you covered in your initial presentation. So tell them what they didn't attend to and repeat the activity (or the step) that gives them the information they need. This approach shows them how to process the information you already presented. A different demonstration or explanation, however, may not show them how to link what you said originally with the new demonstration. So go light on showing children another way.

Because Level B is carefully designed, it is possible to teach all the children the desired behaviors of self-reliance, knowledge about how to follow instructions and the ability to work fast and accurately. If you follow the management rules outlined above, by the time the children have reached lesson 20, all children should be able to complete assigned work within a reasonable period of time, and all should have reasons to feel good about their ability to do the activities.

As they improve, you should tell them about it. "What's this? Everybody's finished with part A already? That's impressive. . . ."

That's what you want to happen. Follow the rules and it will happen.

Tracks

This section shows the development of the major tracks in Level B. The major activities are presented. Part of the discussion includes teaching notes, which address the most common problems teachers encounter.

Classification and Clues

Different classification activities use information or clues to eliminate members of a set until there is only one member of the set remaining. The clues that describe that member have reduced the initial set of possibilities to a very small class—a class with only one possibility.

The different classification activities involve using clues, grouping objects, identifying larger classes and smaller classes, and creating clues to unambiguously identify a particular character or member of a class.

The logic of classification is that some things are in a particular class and some things are not in that class. As the number of things that are in the class grows, the number of things not in the class shrinks. The opposite is also true. As the number of things in the class shrinks, the number of things not in that class grows.

The first classification activities, introduced in lessons 1 through 5, review concepts that had been presented in Level A. Here's part of the activity from lesson 2.

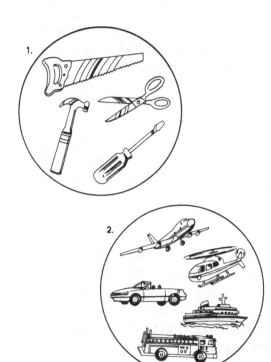

- Touch circle 1. ✔
  The objects in circle 1 are **tools.** Listen: A tool is made to help you do work.
- Touch circle 2. ✔
  The objects in circle 2 are **vehicles.** Listen: A vehicle is made to take things places.
2. Everybody, what is a vehicle made to do? (Signal.) *Take things places.*
- What is a tool made to do? (Signal.) *Help you do work..*
  (Repeat step 2 until firm.)
3. Get ready to play a game. Listen carefully: I'm thinking of an object in one of the circles. I'm going to give you clues.
4. Here's the first clue: The object I'm thinking of is a **tool.** So you know which **circle** it must be in.
- Touch that circle. ✔
5. Here's the next clue: You use this tool to **cut.**
- Everybody, do you **know** which tool I'm thinking of yet? (Signal.) *No.*
- But you should know some tools I could **not** be thinking of.
  I could **not** be thinking of a hammer. Why not? (Call on a child. Idea: *You don't cut with a hammer.*)

- I could **not** be thinking of a screwdriver. Why not? (Call on a child. Idea: *You don't cut with a screwdriver.*)
- I **could** be thinking of the saw because it's a tool and you use a saw to cut. Or I **could** be thinking of scissors.
- How do you know I could be thinking of scissors? (Call on a child. Idea: *It's a tool and you use scissors to cut.*)

6. Here's the next clue: This kind of tool cuts wood.
- Everybody, do you know which tool I'm thinking of yet? (Signal.) *Yes.*
- Which tool? (Signal.) *The saw.*
- Listen: You cut with scissors. How do you know I wasn't thinking of scissors? (Call on a child. Idea: *They don't cut wood.*)

Teaching Notes

Always relate the correct answer to the clue that you give. For instance, you say, "You use this tool to cut." (Step 5) Then you ask the children to indicate why you could not be thinking of a hammer or a screwdriver. Often, children will "sort of" answer these items correctly. When asked how they know that you're not thinking of a hammer, they will say something like, "You pound nails with a hammer."

Do not accept such responses as correct. Say, "Listen: You use this tool to cut. Do you use a hammer to cut?" (Signal.) *"No."*

"That's why I could not be thinking of a hammer. Once more: Tell me why I could not be thinking of a hammer."

Use the specified children's responses to evaluate responses.

Starting in lesson 22, children learn subclasses of dogs. They learn to identify some hounds and some work dogs. By using a "class" box and a "not-class" box, children make different types of classes. Here's the activity from lesson 24.

(**Note:** Children have already learned to identify and group some hounds and some work dogs.)

1. (Write on the board:)

Lesson 24

This says **Lesson 24.**
Open the back cover of your book and touch the column of dogs that has **Lesson 24** on top. Raise your hand when you've found it.
(Observe children and give feedback.)
- You should be touching the column closest to the edge of the page.

2. Some of these dogs are work dogs, and some are hounds.
- Everybody, touch the first dog. ✔
What dog is that? (Signal.) *Collie.*
- What group does a collie belong to? (Signal.) *Work dogs.*
- Touch the next dog. ✔
What dog is that? (Signal.) *Basset.*
- What group does a basset belong to? (Signal.) *Hounds.*

- Touch the next dog. ✔
  What dog is that? (Signal.) *Beagle.*
- What group does a beagle belong to?
  (Signal.) *Hounds.*
- Touch the next dog. ✔
  What dog is that? (Signal.) *Greyhound.*
- What group does a greyhound belong
  to? (Signal.) *Hounds.*
- Touch the next dog. ✔
  What dog is that? (Signal.) *St. Bernard.*
- What group does a St. Bernard belong
  to? (Signal.) *Work dogs.*
- Touch the next dog. ✔
  What dog is that? (Signal.)
  German shepherd.
- What group does a German shepherd
  belong to? (Signal.) *Work dogs.*
3. The rest of the pictures show dogs that
   aren't work dogs and aren't hounds.
- You're going to cut out that column.
  You'll start at the top and cut very
  carefully along the line. Cut carefully,
  because you're going to use this page
  in later lessons. Cut out the whole
  column of dogs. Raise your hand when
  you're finished. ✔
  Now cut out each dog and we'll play a
  tough game. Raise your hand when
  you're finished.

Workbook Activity

Class	Not-Class

- Listen: One of the boxes has the word
  class above it.
- Touch that box. ✔
- The other box has the words **not-class**
  above it.

- Touch that box. ✔
2. You're going to make up different
   classes. You make up a class by
   putting things in the class box. I'll tell
   you the name of the things for a big
   class.
- Listen: Dogs.
- Fix up your class box. Put all the dogs
  in the class box. Raise your hand when
  you're finished.
  (Observe children and give feedback.)
- You should have all the dogs in your
  class box. That's the biggest class you
  can make with your cut-outs.
3. Now you'll make a smaller class by
   putting some dogs in the not-class box.
   Anything in the not-class box is **not** part
   of the class.
- Listen: Move all the cut-outs that are
  not work dogs and **not** hounds to the
  not-class box. Leave all the hounds
  and work dogs in your class box. Raise
  your hand when you're finished.
  (Observe children and give feedback.)
- There should be two groups of dogs in
  the class box now. What are they?
  (Call on a child:) *Hounds and work
  dogs.*
- Yes, now the class box has hounds and
  work dogs.
4. Now you're going to make a smaller
   class.
- Listen: Put all your hounds in the not-
  class box. Don't move the other dogs
  out of the class box. Raise your hand
  when you're finished.
  (Observe children and give feedback.)
- There's a small class of dogs in the
  class box now. What's that class?
  (Signal.) *Work dogs.*
5. Now you're going to make a class that's
   even smaller.
- Listen: Move your St. Bernard and your
  collie to the not-class box. Now there's
  only one kind of dog in the class box.
  What's that? (Signal.) *German
  shepherd.*
- That's a smaller class than the class of
  work dogs.

6. Listen: Make the **biggest class** you can in the class box. Move dogs around so that you have as many dogs as possible in the class box. Raise your hand when you're finished.
   (Observe children and give feedback.)
   - You have a very big class now. Everybody, what's the name of that class? (Signal.) *Dogs.*
7. Now see if you can move just some of the dogs to the not-class box so there are two large groups of dogs in the class box. Raise your hand when you're finished.
   (Observe children and give feedback.)
   - What two large groups are in your class box now? (Signal.) *Work dogs and hounds.*
   - What are the other dogs? (Signal.) *A poodle and a springer spaniel.*
8. Listen: Move one of the groups of dogs out of your class box and put it in the not-class box. Just one of the groups. You can pick either group you want to move. Raise your hand when you're finished.
   (Observe children and give feedback.)
   - Now you should have a pretty small class.
9. Raise your hand if your class box has just hounds in it.
   - Everybody with hounds in your class box, where are the work dogs? (Signal.) *In the not-class box.*
   - Where are the other two dogs? (Signal.) *In the not-class box.*
10. Raise your hand if your class box has just **work dogs** in it.
    - Everybody with work dogs in your class box, where are your hounds? (Signal.) *In the not-class box.*
    - Where are the other two dogs? (Signal.) *In the not-class box.*

11. Listen: You're going to make the class so small that it has only one kind of dog in it. Move all the dogs but one of them to the not-class box. Raise your hand when you're finished.
    (Observe children and give feedback.)
    - You should have one dog in the class box and all the others in the not-class box. What does your class box show? (Call on different children. Praise appropriate responses.)
    - You're making up bigger and smaller classes. Good for you.

Teaching Notes

The activity shows the children the relationship between things that are in the class, things that are not in the class and all the things that you are considering. For this activity, the children are considering their cut-out dogs. For the biggest class, all cut-outs, are in the "class" box, and the class is dogs. To make a smaller class, some of the things from the "class" box move to the "not-class" box. The smallest class that can be made with the cut-outs is a single dog.

If children are firm on the relationship between the size of the class and the objects in the class, repeat steps 6 through 11. Tell children to listen carefully and work quickly. Praise children who follow your directions.

Beginning in lesson 32, children mentally manipulate the "class" and "not-class" box. Here's the first part of the exercise from lesson 32.

Class

_____ hounds

_____ fast-running hounds

_____ dogs

_____ animals

This picture shows a class. It doesn't show the not-class box.
- Listen: Raise your hand when you know the name of the smallest class shown in the class box.
- Everybody, what's the class? (Signal.) *Hounds.*
2. You're going to play the great thinking game. **Pretend** that you're going to change the class.
- Listen: You have hounds in the class box. But you want fast-running hounds in the class box. Just fast-running hounds. Think big. Raise your hand when you know whether you add things or take things out of the class box. ✔
3. Everybody, what do you do to the class box? (Signal.) *Take things out.* (Repeat step 3 until firm.)

4. Everybody, which class is smaller, **hounds** or **fast-running hounds**? (Signal.) *Fast-running hounds.*
- How do you know that the class of fast-running hounds is smaller? (Call on a child. Idea: *There are fewer things in the class of fast-running hounds.*)
- The class of fast-running hounds is smaller than the class of hounds. So you'll have to take things out of the class of hounds to get fast-running hounds.
- Listen: If you had the class of fast-running hounds in the class box, which dog would be in your class box? (Signal.) *The greyhound.*
- Where would the beagle and the basset be? (Signal.) *In the not-class box.*
5. New game: You have the class of hounds, but you want the class of **dogs.** Raise your hand when you know whether you'd add things or take things out.
- Everybody, what would you do to change the class box from hounds to dogs? (Signal.) *Add things.*
- Which class is bigger, hounds or dogs? (Signal.) *Dogs.*
- How do you know that the class of dogs is bigger? (Call on a child. Idea: *There are more things in the class of dogs.*)

Teaching Notes

If children incorrectly answer questions you present in steps 3 through 5, correct them by referring to the mental picture they should have of how to change the "class" box. For instance, in step 3 children do not respond firmly when you ask what you do to the "class" box (change it from the class of hounds to the class of fast-running hounds).

"You have hounds, but you want fast-running hounds. Are all the things in the class box fast-running hounds?" (Signal.) *"No."*

"Where would the other things have to go?" (Signal.) *"To the not-class box."*

"So would your class box have more things or fewer things than it does now?" (Signal.) *"Fewer."*

Following mistakes on a "thinking game," repeat the game (steps 2–4 or step 5). Praise children for responding quickly and correctly.

Starting in lesson 35, children learn how additional information about a class member can reduce the membership of the class.

This activity is quite similar to the "mystery object" activities presented in Level A and in Level B. (See Classification and Clues.)

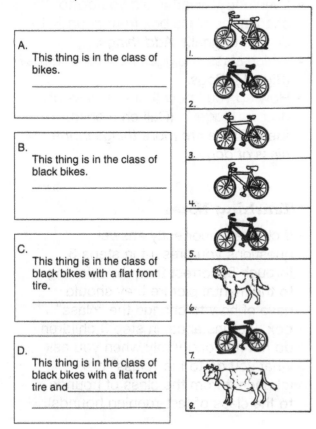

A.
This thing is in the class of bikes.
_____

B.
This thing is in the class of black bikes.
_____

C.
This thing is in the class of black bikes with a flat front tire.
_____

D.
This thing is in the class of black bikes with a flat front tire and_____
_____

The pictures show different bikes. The sentences tell about the classes.
• I'll read the sentences. Follow along.
• Touch sentence A. ✔
This thing is in the class of bikes.
That's the big class.
• Touch sentence B.
This thing is the class of black bikes.
That's a smaller class.
• Touch sentence C.
This thing is in the class of black bikes with a flat front tire.

2. Here's what you're going to do. Below each sentence, write the number of every picture that sentence tells about.
• Touch sentence A. ✔
This thing is in the class of bikes. You have to write the number of every picture that sentence tells about. You'll write the number of every picture that shows a bike.
• Picture 1 shows a bike, so you'd write number 1 on the line below sentence A.
• Picture 2 shows a bike, so you'd write number 2 under the sentence.
• Listen: Write the number of every picture that shows a bike. Raise your hand when you're finished.
(Observe children and give feedback.)
• (Write on the board:)

1, 2, 3, 4, 5, 7

• Here are the numbers you should have under sentence A—1, 2, 3, 4, 5, 7. Raise your hand if you got it right.
• Everybody, look at picture number 6.
• Why didn't you write that number under the first sentence? (Call on individual children. Idea: *A St. Bernard is not a bike.*)
• Everybody, what other number didn't you write? (Signal.) *8.*
• Why didn't you write the number for Clarabelle? (Call on a child. Idea: *She's not a bike.*)

3. Touch sentence B.
This thing is in the class of **black** bikes. Is that class bigger or smaller than the class of bikes? (Signal.) *Smaller.*
- So you should have fewer things in this class.
- Write the number of everything that's in the class of **black** bikes. Raise your hand when you're finished.
(Observe children and give feedback.)
- (Write on the board:)

2,5,7

- Here are the numbers you should have for the things in the class of black bikes. Raise your hand if you got it right.
4. Touch sentence C.
This thing is in the class of black bikes with a flat front tire. Remember, it's in the class of **black** bikes with a flat front tire, not just any old bike with a flat front tire. Write the numbers for the things in that class. Raise your hand when you're finished.
(Observe children and give feedback.)
- Everybody, which things are in the class of black bikes with a flat front tire? (Signal.) *5 and 7.*
- There are two things in that class, but we're going to tell about only one thing.
- Touch **only** bike 5. ✔
That's the bike with the flat front tire you'll tell about.
5. Touch sentence D.
It says: This thing is in the class of black bikes with a flat front tire and . . . something else.
- You're going to complete that sentence so it tells about bike 5 and **no other** bike that's black and has a flat front tire.
- Look at the picture of bike 5. See what else you can say about that bike and write it. That bike has a flat front tire and something else. Raise your hand when you're finished.
(Observe children and give feedback.)

- (Call on different children to read their sentence. Praise sentences that tell about a flat rear tire. Say:) That's a really super sentence: Raise your hand if you wrote that super sentence.
(Praise sentences that tell about a flat rear tire.)
- This is pretty hard, but a lot of you are too smart to get fooled.

Starting in lesson 60, children write three sentences to identify a "mystery character." Each clue the children construct is designed to eliminate one or more possibility. Here's the activity from lesson 60.

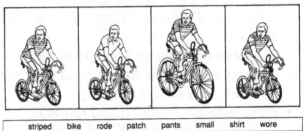

striped   bike   rode   patch   pants   small   shirt   wore

You're going to use lined paper and write clues that tell about the mystery man.
2. The mystery man is in the first picture.
- Touch that man.
Make sure you're touching the right man or you'll make silly clues.
- All your clues should tell something that you can't say about all the men. Here's a bad clue: The man rode a bike. Why is that a bad clue? (Call on a child. Idea: *All the men rode a bike.*)
- Here's a good clue: The man had a patch on his pants. Why is that a good clue? (Call on a child. Idea: *Not all the men had a patch on their pants.*)
- Who can say another good clue? (Call on a child. Accept clues such as: *The man rode a small bike; The man wore a striped shirt.*)
3. (Write on the board:)

The man _____.

- You're going to write three clues. Somebody who reads all three clues would know exactly which man was the mystery man.
- Each clue will start with the words **the man.** Each clue will tell what the man wore or did.
- Touch the vocabulary box below the picture. I'll read the words: striped . . . bike . . . rode . . . patch . . . pants . . . small . . . shirt . . . wore.
- If you use any of those words, spell them correctly. Write your three clues. Remember the capital at the beginning and the period at the end of each sentence. Raise your hand when you're finished.
  (Observe children and give feedback.)
4. (Call on several children to read their set of clues. For each child, say:)
- Read your first clue. (Child reads.)
- Read your next clue. (Child reads.)
- Read your last clue. (Child reads.)
- (For each child, ask:)
  Everybody, do those three clues let you know which man is the mystery man? (Children respond.)
- (Praise good sets of clues.)

> **Key:** Good sets contain these 3 ideas in any order.
> *The man rode a small bike.*
> *The man wore a striped shirt.*
> *The man had a patch on his pants.*

Teaching Note

Earlier in the program, children learned about clues by working with sequences that showed a series of events over time. These sequences served to teach children the role of clues. (See Temporal Sequencing.) As a **group,** the clues should lead to the identification of only one character or one sequence. **Individually,** each good clue rules out one or more possibilities.

Temporal Sequencing

The activities on temporal sequencing are important for several reasons.

1. They present a picture sequence that corresponds to a sequence of events in time. When working with the sequence, children strengthen their understanding of this relationship.

2. The tasks present sentences that are temporally "backward." "Dud went tracking after he ate a ham bone." The first event that occurred in time was Dud eating a ham bone. However, this event is not named first in the sentence. Work with sentences of this type is important for the understanding of many things that are described in science and social studies.

3. The sequences lend themselves to many types of activities that involve "the mystery sequence." Level B first introduces temporal sequences in lesson 27. Children work from a sequence of pictures that show which events occurred first, next and last. Children complete sentences that use the word "after."

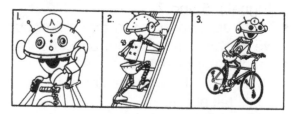

1. Bleep climbed a ladder after he _____
   _____.
2. Bleep rode a bike after he _____
   _____.

1. These pictures show what Bleep did first, next and last.
- Touch the first picture.
  Everybody, what did Bleep do first? (Signal.) *Talked on the phone.*
- Touch picture 2.
  That picture shows what Bleep did **after** he talked on the phone.
- What did he do after he talked on the phone? (Signal.) *Climbed a ladder.*

- Yes, Bleep climbed a ladder **after** he talked on the phone.
- Touch picture 3.
  That picture shows what Bleep did after he climbed a ladder.
- What did he do after he climbed a ladder? (Signal.) *Rode a bike.*
- Yes, Bleep rode a bike after he climbed a ladder.

2. Touch the picture of Bleep riding a bike. Listen: Bleep rode a bike after he did something else. He rode a bike after he did what? (Signal.) *Climbed a ladder.*

3. I'll start with **Bleep rode a bike** and tell when he did that. Listen: Bleep rode a bike after he climbed a ladder.
- Your turn: Start with **Bleep rode a bike** and tell when. Get ready. (Signal.) *Bleep rode a bike after he climbed a ladder.*
  (Repeat step 3 until firm.)

4. Touch the picture of Bleep climbing a ladder. Listen: Bleep climbed a ladder after he did something else. Bleep climbed a ladder after he did what? (Signal.) *Talked on the phone.*

5. I'll start with **Bleep climbed a ladder** and tell when he did that. Listen: Bleep climbed a ladder after he talked on the phone.
- Your turn: Start with **Bleep climbed a ladder** and tell when. Get ready. (Signal.) *Bleep climbed a ladder after he talked on the phone.*
  (Repeat step 5 until firm.)

6. (Write on the board:)

   talked on the phone
   climbed a ladder
   rode a bike

- You're going to complete sentences. You'll have to pick the right part. I'll read each part: (**Point to each part and read it.**)

7. Touch sentence 1 below the pictures. It says: Bleep climbed a ladder after he . . . He climbed a ladder after he did something else. Write that something else. Raise your hand when you're finished.
   (**Observe children and give feedback.**)

8. Here's what you should have for sentence 1: Bleep climbed a ladder after he talked on the phone. Raise your hand if you got it right.

9. Touch sentence 2.
   It says: Bleep rode a bike after he . . . He rode a bike just after he did something else. Write that something else. Raise your hand when you're finished.
   (**Observe children and give feedback.**)

10. Here's what you should have for sentence 2: Bleep rode a bike after he climbed a ladder. Raise your hand if you got sentence 2 right.
- Raise both your hands if you got both sentences right.
- Those are very tricky sentences.

For sentence 1, children find the picture of Bleep climbing a ladder. They observe that Bleep climbed the ladder after he did something else. They describe that something else.

The next format presents children with a series of "arrows" that show different orders of events. The teacher gives clues about the mystery sequence. Children circle pictures for each clue. Each clue rules out one or more of the sequences. The first exercise appears in lesson 37.

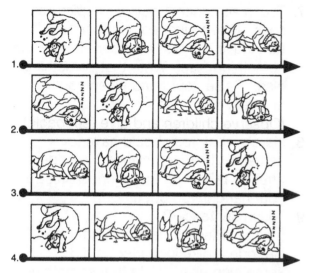

1. These four arrows show different things that Dud did.
  - I'll give you clues. You'll figure out which arrows the clues tell about. To do that, you'll circle pictures I tell about.
2. Touch arrow 1. ✔
  The first picture shows Dud somersaulting in the snow. What did he do just after he somersaulted? (Signal.) *Ate a ham bone.*
  - Yes, he ate a ham bone.
  - What did he do just after he ate a ham bone? (Signal.) *Slept.*
  - That last picture shows him tracking in the snow. That's what he did just after he slept.
3. Touch arrow 2.
  What did Dud do first? (Signal.) *Slept.*
  - What did he do after he slept? (Signal.) *Somersaulted.*
  - What did he do after he somersaulted in the snow? (Signal.) *Tracked.*
  - What did he do after he tracked in the snow? (Signal.) *Ate a ham bone.*
4. I'm thinking about one of the arrows on this page. Here's the clue about the arrow I'm thinking of: On this arrow, Dud ate a ham bone just after he tracked in the snow.
  - Find the first arrow that shows Dud ate a ham bone just **after** he tracked in the snow. Raise your hand when you know the first arrow with those pictures.

- Everybody, what's the number of the first arrow that shows Dud eating a ham bone just after he tracked in the snow? (Signal.) *Two.*
- (Draw on the board:)

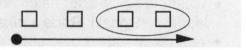

- The picture on the board shows what you do on arrow 2. You draw one big circle around the pictures that show **Dud ate a ham bone just after he tracked in the snow.**
- Make your circle on arrow 2. Then find any other arrows that show **Dud ate a ham bone just after he tracked in the snow** and circle the pictures. Raise your hand when you're finished. **(Observe children and give feedback.)**
- Everybody, did you draw a circle around the pictures on arrow 3? (Signal.) *Yes.*
- Yes, the first two pictures on arrow 3 show Dud eating a ham bone just after he tracked in the snow. So you should have a circle around the first two pictures.
- Everybody, did you draw a circle around the pictures on arrow 4? (Signal.) *Yes.*
- Yes, the middle two pictures on arrow 4 show Dud eating a ham bone just after he tracked in the snow. So you should have a circle around the middle two pictures.
- Raise your hand if you have a circle on arrow 2, arrow 3 and arrow 4.
- The mystery arrow could be any arrow that shows Dud eating a ham bone just after he tracked in the snow. One of the arrows could not be the mystery arrow. Raise your hand when you know which arrow could not be the mystery arrow.
- Everybody, which arrow? (Signal.) *One.*
- Draw a line through the pictures on arrow 1 because it couldn't be the mystery arrow. Raise your hand when you're finished. ✔

5. Here's clue 2 about the mystery arrow: The mystery arrow shows Dud sleeping just after he ate a ham bone.
- Look at the arrows that are not crossed out. Draw a circle around the picture of **Dud sleeping just after he ate a ham bone.** Don't get fooled. Find him sleeping just after eating and circle him sleeping. Raise your hand when you're finished.
  (Observe children and give feedback.)
- You should have circled Dud sleeping on two arrows. What's the first arrow that shows Dud sleeping just after he ate a ham bone? (Signal.) *Three.*
- What's the other arrow that shows Dud sleeping just after he ate a ham bone? (Signal.) *Four.*
- You can cross out one more arrow because it doesn't show both clues about Dud. Raise your hand when you know the new arrow you can cross out. ✔
- Everybody, which arrow? (Signal.) *Two.*
- Draw a line through the pictures on arrow 2. It couldn't be the mystery arrow. It shows Dud eating a ham bone just after he tracked in the snow, but it doesn't show Dud sleeping just after he ate a ham bone.

6. Here's the last clue. Listen: the mystery arrow shows Dud somersaulting in the snow just after he slept. Listen again: The mystery arrow shows Dud somersaulting in the snow just after he slept.
- Circle any picture that shows Dud somersaulting just after he slept. Raise your hand when you're finished.
  (Observe children and give feedback.)
- You should have circled Dud somersaulting just after he slept on arrow 3.
- Now cross out any arrow that could not be the mystery arrow. Raise your hand when you're finished. ✔

- You should have crossed out arrow 4. Now you know the mystery arrow. It's the only arrow not crossed out. Everybody, which arrow is the mystery arrow? (Signal.) *Three.*
- Here's a tough question: Why couldn't arrow 4 be the mystery arrow? (Call on a child. Idea: *It doesn't show Dud somersaulting in the snow just after he slept.*)

7. Raise your hand if you followed all the clues and found the mystery arrow. Good for you.

Teaching Notes

Some children may make "reversals." For instance, in step 5, children may circle the pictures on arrow 2. To correct reversal problems, say the sentence. Then prompt the "after" relationship.

For example. "Listen: Dud was sleeping just after he ate a ham bone. He was sleeping just after he did something else. What did he do first? Find the right pictures."

The teacher script indicates that children should circle a single picture for clue 2 (step 5). Part of the reason for this specification is that children have trouble if their circles overlap (which is what happens on arrow 3 and arrow 4). The following is the workbook answer key for this exercise, showing how the children's workbooks should look.

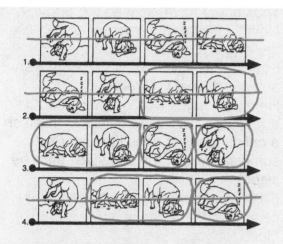

If children become confused, introduce a variation of the procedure in which children use different-colored crayons for circling different clues. For the first clue (step 4), children circle the **two pictures** with a red crayon. For the second clue, they circle **two pictures** with their blue crayon. They use a black crayon for their third clue. Below is the workbook answer key using different-colored crayons.

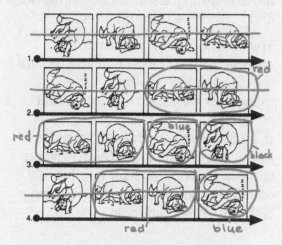

This activity is very sophisticated, but the children will do it if you take them through it a step at a time just as it is specified in the exercise. If children have trouble, post some of the better worksheets and praise the children who performed correctly.

A variation of temporal sequencing is introduced in lesson 51. For this variation, a single picture sequence is presented. Children complete two clues that tell about the sequence.

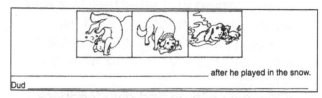

after he played in the snow.

Dud _____

1. (Write on the board:)

> **Dud he after snow the ate went in ham bone played swimming**

- Open your workbook to lesson 51 and find part A. The pictures show Dud doing three things.
- Touch the first thing Dud did. ✔ What did Dud do first? (Signal.) *Played in the snow.*
- Touch the next thing Dud did. What did Dud do after he played in the snow? (Signal.) *Ate a ham bone.*
- Touch the last thing Dud did. What did Dud do after he ate a ham bone? (Signal.) *Went swimming.*

2. You're going to complete sentences that tell what Dud did after he played in the snow and what he did after he ate a ham bone.

- (Point to the words on the board.) Here are some words you may use. (Touch each word as you say:) Dud, he, after, snow, the, ate, went, in, ham bone, played, swimming. If you use any of those words, make sure you spell them correctly.

3. Touch number 1. ✔

- On that line, you'll write what Dud did after he played in the snow.
- Touch the picture that shows what Dud did after he played in the snow. ✔
- Start your sentence with **Dud** and tell what he did after he played in the snow. Raise your hand when you're finished. (Observe children and give feedback.)

4. (Write on the board:)

> **Dud ate a ham bone after he played in the snow.**

- Here's what you should have for your first sentence: Dud ate a ham bone after he played in the snow. Raise your hand if you wrote everything correctly.

5. Touch number 2. ✔
- You'll write the whole sentence that tells what Dud did after he ate a ham bone.
- Touch the picture that shows what Dud did after he ate a ham bone. ✔
- The word **Dud** is already written. Tell what Dud did in the last picture. Then tell when he did it. Remember, Dud went swimming **after** he ate a ham bone. Raise your hand when you're finished.
(Observe children and give feedback.)

6. (Write on the board:)

> **Dud went swimming after he ate a ham bone.**

- Here's what you should have for your second sentence.
- Raise your hand if you wrote everything correctly and if you put a period at the end of the sentence.

A later variation of the sentence-writing activity is presented in lessons 56 and 57. Children are presented with a group of sequences. They are assigned to write clues for one of the arrows. They write two clues. The first describes what occurred in the first two pictures. The next clue tells what happened in the second and third pictures.

Deductions

Deductions are important for work in science and social studies. Deductions are often assumed in everyday exchanges. Although children are familiar with the events and the logic, they are often unfamiliar with the verbal expression of the logic. For instance, they may have serious problems completing the last sentence in this item: "Everybody who works at the spa is in good shape. Debby works at the spa. So Debby . . . " To us, the last sentence is obvious: So Debby is in good shape. A very common response that children make, however, is: "*So Debby works at the spa.*"

Their mistake shows that they don't understand the basic pattern game assumed by deductions. The game is to recombine the information that is given to come up with something that is new—to draw a conclusion.

Teachers often dislike work with inference and deductions because the material is difficult for the children and even more difficult to explain. Level B of *Reasoning and Writing* presents deductions in a way that children learn very quickly how they work.

The method involves putting the information on three arrows:

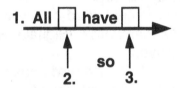

The top arrow presents the "rule." Arrows 2 and 3 apply the rule. These arrows tell about the two boxes on the top arrow. Arrow 2 gives information that something is in the class of things in the first box. Arrow 3 gives information that the same thing is in the class of things shown in the second box.

Exercises with deductions begin in lesson 8.
Here's the introductory exercise.

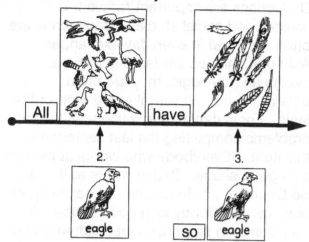

You're going to learn to say a 3-arrow deduction. This is tough, tough, tough.

2. (Draw on the board:)

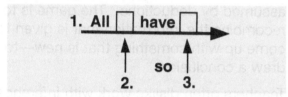

• (Touch arrow 1.) The first word on your arrow is **All.** Touch the word **All.** ✔
• Now touch the picture just after the word **All.**
• Everybody, what's in that picture? (Signal.) *Birds.*
• So the first part of the arrow rule is: **All birds.** What's the first part? (Signal.) *All birds.*

3. Touch the next word on arrow 1. What's that word? (Signal.) *Have.*
• Yes, **have.**
• So the rule is: **All birds have . . .**

4. Touch the last picture. ✔
The last picture shows what all birds have. What do all birds have? (Signal.) *Feathers.*
• **I'll** say the rule for arrow 1. **You** touch the things I say. Here we go: All . . . ✔
birds . . . ✔
have . . . ✔
feathers. ✔

5. Everybody, say the rule for arrow 1. (Signal.) *All birds have feathers.*
(Repeat step 5 until firm.)

6. Now touch the first arrow that goes **up.** That's arrow 2. ✔
• (Touch arrow 2.)

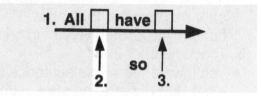

• Here's the arrow you should be touching.
• There's a picture at the bottom of arrow 2. What's in that picture? (Signal.) *An eagle.*
• Arrow 2 shows that the eagle belongs in the first picture. **An eagle is a bird.** That's the rule for arrow 2: An eagle is a bird.

7. Everybody, say that rule. (Signal.) *An eagle is a bird.*
(Repeat step 7 until firm.)

8. Touch the last arrow that goes **up.** That's arrow 3. ✔
• (Touch arrow 3.)

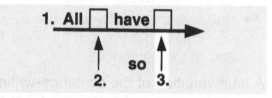

• Here's the arrow you should be touching.
• What's at the bottom of that arrow? (Signal.) *An eagle.*
Yes, it's an eagle again.
• The word next to that eagle is **so.** Touch the word **so.** ✔
What's that word? (Signal.) *So.*
Now go up arrow 3 and you'll see what the eagle has.
What does the eagle have? (Signal.) *Feathers.*
• Here's the rule for arrow 3: **So an eagle has feathers.**

9. Say that rule. (Signal.) *So an eagle has feathers.*
(Repeat step 9 until firm.)

10. I'm going to say the rule for all the arrows. I'll start with arrow 1.
    - (Touch arrow 1 on the board.) Listen: **All birds have feathers.**
    - (Touch arrow 2.) **An eagle is a bird.**
    - (Touch arrow 3.) **So an eagle has feathers.**
11. Once more.
    - (Touch arrow 1.) **All birds have feathers.**
    - (Touch arrow 2.) **An eagle is a bird.**
    - (Touch arrow 3.) **So an eagle has feathers.**
12. Let's see if you can say the whole deduction. I'll tell you which arrow to touch. You say the statement for that arrow. Remember, you have to say the word **so** just before you say the statement for the last arrow.
13. Touch arrow 1. ✔
    Say the statement. (Signal.) *All birds have feathers.*
    - Touch arrow 2. ✔
    Say the statement. (Signal.) *An eagle is a bird.*
    - Touch arrow 3. ✔
    Say the statement. (Signal.) *So an eagle has feathers.*
    (Repeat step 13 until firm.)
14. See if you can say the whole thing. Remember, say the statement for arrow 1, then arrow 2, then arrow 3. Get ready. (Signal.) *All birds have feathers. An eagle is a bird. So an eagle has feathers.*
    (Repeat step 14 until firm.)
15. Raise your hand if you can say the whole deduction. (Call on a child. Praise correct response.)

Teaching Notes

Rehearse this format before you present it. If you know the steps and can deliver your lines fluently, the children will catch on quickly.

Make sure you firm the different statements that children are to make. You are to firm in steps 5, 7, 9, 13 and 14.

Expect the first part of the exercise (through step 9) to move slowly. The last part (steps 10–15) should go fast. Make sure you hold children to a very high criterion of performance in steps 13 and 14. Position yourself where you can observe what children are pointing to and what they are saying.

Make a fuss over children who can say the whole deduction correctly (step 15).

If children are firm in this exercise, they will move through later exercises very quickly.

Variations of picture deductions are presented in lessons following lesson 8. A generically different type of deduction is introduced in lesson 25. Children construct a deduction to answer questions. This activity is similar to the one facing a story character, Sherlock, who is trying to solve a mystery and answer a question.

Here's the first part of the activity from lesson 25. In this exercise, children write deductions for three questions. Here's the part of the exercise that deals with the first question.

toadstools

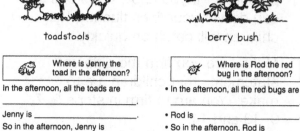

berry bush

Where is Jenny the toad in the afternoon?	Where is Rod the red bug in the afternoon?
In the afternoon, all the toads are _____	• In the afternoon, all the red bugs are _____
Jenny is _____.	• Rod is _____
So in the afternoon, Jenny is _____	• So in the afternoon, Rod is _____

1. Everybody, you're going to need these crayons: red and brown. Take them out. Raise your hand when you're ready. ✔
   - Find part C.
   This picture shows the afternoon, but not everything is shown in the picture.
2. Touch the toadstools. ✔
   - Here's the rule about the toadstools: In the afternoon, all the toads are on toadstools.
   - Fix up your toadstools so they have brown toads on them. Raise your hand when you're finished.
   (Observe children and give feedback.)
3. Touch the box with the picture of the toad. ✔
   That's Jenny the toad.
   - Touch the question in that box. ✔
   - I'll read it: Where is Jenny the toad in the afternoon?
   - Everybody, what does that question say? **(Signal.)** *Where is Jenny the toad in the afternoon?*
   - You're going to tell about Jenny by completing the deduction below the box.

   - Touch the first part of that deduction. ✔
   The first part says: In the afternoon, all the toads are . . .
   - Where are all the toads? **(Signal.)** *On toadstools.*
   - So the first sentence should say: In the afternoon, all the toads are **on toadstools.**
   - Complete the first sentence. Raise your hand when you're finished. ✔
4. Touch the next sentence. ✔
   It says: Jenny is . . .
   - What is Jenny? **(Signal.)** *A toad.*
   - Finish that sentence. Raise your hand when you're finished. ✔
5. Now you can complete the last sentence. It says: So in the afternoon, Jenny is . . .
   - Complete that sentence. Tell where Jenny is in the afternoon. Don't make the same kind of mistake the gray rat makes. Raise your hand when you're finished. ✔
   - Here's what you should have for the last sentence: So in the afternoon, Jenny is on a toadstool. Raise your hand if you got it right.
6. So you answered the question about Jenny. Where is Jenny in the afternoon? **(Signal.)** *On a toadstool.*
   - And you wrote a deduction to tell how you figured it out.
   - I can say the whole deduction: In the afternoon, all the toads are on toadstools. Jenny is a toad. So in the afternoon, Jenny is on a toadstool.
   - Who thinks they can say that whole deduction without looking? **(Call on several children. For each correct deduction, say:)** You're sure a lot better at figuring things out than the gray rat is.

Teaching Notes

Although the wording for these deductions is slightly different from that presented earlier, children should have no trouble because the format of ordering the sentences is the same as that for earlier deductions.

In step 6, you call on different children to say the whole deduction about Jenny. If the children you call on tend to have trouble, say the whole deduction for the class and direct them to say the whole deduction together. Then call on several children to make sure that they are firm.

In lesson 39, children are introduced to deductions that are formally invalid. They are invalid because they do not present the three sentences in the appropriate order (1, 2, 3). Instead, they present them in this order: 1, 3, 2. The exercise in lesson 39 follows an episode of Sherlock in which he formulates invalid deductions.

1. (Draw on the board:)

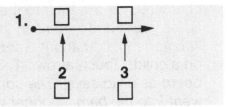

- I'll show you why Sherlock's deduction about who stole the corn doesn't work.
- For a good deduction, you do arrow 1, then arrow 2, then arrow 3. If you do the arrows in the wrong order, the deduction just doesn't work.
- Sherlock's deduction doesn't work because it does arrow 1, then arrow 3, then arrow 2.
2. Everybody, find part C.
Touch arrow 1.
Here's the rule for that arrow: The corn thief went into the barn. Everybody, say that sentence. **(Signal.)** *The corn thief went into the barn.*
- Sherlock's first sentence says: The corn thief went into the barn. His next sentence should tell who the corn thief is. That's arrow 2. But he did arrow 3, not arrow 2. He told who went into the barn.
- Touch arrow 3.
Here's the statement for that arrow: The red chicken went into the barn.
- Touch arrow 2.
So the red chicken is the corn thief.
3. I'll say his whole deduction. Touch the arrows.
- The corn thief went into the barn.
- The red chicken went into the barn.
- So the red chicken is the corn thief.
4. You say his whole deduction. I'll touch the arrows on the board.
- First sentence. **(Touch arrow 1.)** *The corn thief went into the barn.*
- Next sentence. **(Touch arrow 3.)** *The red chicken went into the barn.*
- Last sentence. **(Touch arrow 2.)** *So the red chicken is the corn thief.*
- That's wrong.

5. Below the arrows are some pictures of characters who went into the barn. Raise your hand if you can say the wrong deduction about Goober. (Call on a child. Touch arrows 1, 3, 2 on board as child says: *The corn thief went into the barn. Goober went into the barn. So Goober is the corn thief.*) Yes, that's not a good deduction.
   - Raise your hand if you can say a wrong deduction about Sherlock. (Call on a child. Touch arrows on the board as the child says the deduction.)
   - Yes, that's a mixed-up deduction.
6. Sherlock's deduction is all mixed up. But listen to how silly it would sound if he put the sentences in the right order. I'll do arrows 1, 2 and 3 in the right order. Listen:
   - (Touch arrow 1.)
     The corn thief went into the barn.
   - (Touch arrow 2.)
     The red chicken is the corn thief.
   - (Touch arrow 3.)
     So the red chicken went into the barn.
   - No matter how you look at it, Sherlock is pretty mixed up.

Later in the program, children work with and construct deductions that are formally wrong.

Dialect

Starting in lesson 6 and continuing through lesson 59, children work on different *dialect* activities. The term *dialect* refers to speech that is transformed through a very specific change in the pronunciation of a particular sound. Regular talk can be transformed into dialect by changing the letters for the transformed sound in the dialect.

Different dialect exercises are presented. Each reinforces reading and pronunciation skills while it teaches a new sound game that children can extend to situations beyond the instructional context.

The first dialect exercise follows a story in which Bleep (a robot) adjusts his speaking mechanism so that he says the short **u** sound instead of the short **e** sound. Here's the exercise that follows the Bleep story in lesson 7.

1. Bleep said some strange things in this story. See if you know what he was trying to say.
   - Listen: Bleep said, "I want to talk butter." Everybody, say that. (Signal.) *I want to talk butter.*
   - Now say what Bleep was trying to say. (Signal.) *I want to talk better.*
2. Listen: Bleep said, "There is no stamp on this lutter." Everybody, say that. (Signal.) *There is no stamp on this lutter.*
   Now say what Bleep was trying to say. (Signal.) *There is no stamp on this letter.*
3. Listen: Bleep said, "I will gut a stamp." Everybody, say that. (Signal.) *I will gut a stamp.*
   - Now say what Bleep was trying to say. (Signal.) *I will get a stamp.*
4. Here's a tough one. Listen: Bleep said, "Hullo, Bun." Everybody, say that. (Signal.) *Hullo, Bun.*
   - Now say what Bleep was trying to say. (Signal.) *Hello, Ben.*
5. I'll say some other things Bleep might say. You tell me what he was trying to say.
   - Listen: It's time to rust. Everybody, say it. (Signal.) *It's time to rust.*
   - Now say what Bleep was trying to say. (Signal.) *It's time to rest.*
   - Listen: Molly sleeps in a bud. Everybody, say it. (Signal.) *Molly sleeps in a bud.*
   - Now say what Bleep was trying to say. (Signal.) *Molly sleeps in a bed.*

Workbook Activity

1. bud   2. yus   3. fud   4. ugg

_____ _____ _____ _____

1. These are words that Bleep said. You're going to write the words Bleep was trying to say.
2. Everybody, touch word 1. ✔
   - That word is **bud.** What word? (Signal.) *Bud.*
   - What word was Bleep trying to say? (Signal.) *Bed.*
   - Write the word **bed** below the word **bud.** Raise your hand when you're finished.
   - (Write on the board:)

   bed

   - Check your work. Here's the word Bleep was trying to say. Raise your hand if you got it right.

3. Touch word 2. ✔
   - That word is **yus.** What word was Bleep trying to say? (Signal.) *Yes.*
   - Write the word **yes** below the word **yus.** Raise your hand when you're finished.
   - (Write on the board:)

   yes

   - Check your work. Here's the word you should have written below **yus.** Raise your hand if you got it right.
4. Touch word 3. ✔
   - That word is **fud.** What word was Bleep trying to say? (Signal.) *Fed.*
   - Write the word **fed** below the word **fud.** Raise your hand when you're finished.
   - (Write on the board:)

   fed

   - Check your work. Here's what you should have written below **fud.** Raise your hand if you got it right.
5. Touch word 4. ✔
   - That word is **ugg.** What word was Bleep trying to say? (Signal.) *Egg.*
   - Write the word **egg** below the word **ugg.** Raise your hand when you're finished.
   - (Write on the board:)

   egg

   - Check your work. Here's the word you should have written below **ugg.** Raise your hand if you got it right.
6. Raise your hand if you got all the words right. You're really good at figuring out what Bleep was trying to say.

In later exercises, children convert "regular" speech into "Bleep-talk." Different dialects are presented. One involves "non-nasal" talk. Here's an exercise from lesson 49.

This picture shows what would have happened if the big wind hadn't started blowing from the east at the end of the story.
- Molly is at the top of the basement stairs. See if you can read what she's saying.
- What is Molly saying? (Call on a child.) *Bleep, are you almost finished?*
- And Bleep is answering. Everybody, what is Bleep saying? (Signal.) *Yes.*
- That's what would have happened if the great wind hadn't started blowing.
- But when the wind started blowing, Molly had to wear something to protect her from the smell. What's that? (Signal.) *A clothespin.*
- And when she wore the clothespin, she couldn't say some of the words the right way. Raise your hand when you know which words she couldn't say.
- What's the first word she couldn't say? (Signal.) *Almost.*
- What's the next word she couldn't say? (Signal.) *Finished.*

2. Underline the word **almost** and the word **finished**. Then fix up those words so they say what Molly actually said with the clothespin on her nose. Cross out the letters she can't say. Write the letter she said above it.
- (Write on the board:)

	b		d	
	al~~m~~ost		fi~~n~~ished	

- Here's what you should have.
3. Raise your hand if you remember what Bleep always said when he heard people talking in that strange way. Everybody, what did he say? (Signal.) *Blurp.*
4. Fix up Bleep so he says **blurp**.
- Cross out the word **yes** and write **blurp**. Raise your hand when you're finished.
- (Write on the board:)

Blurp

- Here's what you should have.
- Later you can fix up that picture so it shows a clothespin on Molly's nose.

Directions (North, South, East, West)

The work on directions proceeds in three phases. First, children learn to face different directions in the classroom. Next, children learn the code for maps. (North is at the top; south at the bottom.) Finally, children engage in a variety of exercises that involve following instructions for getting to different places on a map or creating instructions. These instructions involve relative directions. (The place is north of something but south of something else.)

The concepts that are taught in the Directions track are important for children, both in terms of communication skills that are taught and in terms of the knowledge that makes future work in science and social studies easier and more comprehensible.

The work with directions begins in lesson 5 and continues through lesson 62. Here's part of the exercise from lesson 5.

5. I put the letters for directions on two walls.
- When I face **north,** I face the wall with **N** on it. Watch. **(Face the N wall.)** I'm facing north.
- Everybody, stand up.
6. Your turn: Face **north.** Get ready. Go. ✔
  Which direction are you facing? (Signal.) *North.*
- Listen: When you face **north, south** is behind you.
- Everybody, face **south.** Get ready. Go. ✔
  Which direction are you facing? (Signal.) *South.*
  (Repeat step 6 until firm.)
- Everybody, sit down.
7. I'll point to a wall. You tell me which direction I'm pointing.
- **(Point south.)**
  Everybody, which direction am I pointing? (Signal.) *South.*
- **(Point north.)**
  Which direction am I pointing? (Signal.) *North.*
8. Your turn: Everybody, point **south.** Get ready. Go. ✔
- Point **north.** Get ready. Go. ✔
  (Repeat step 8 until firm.)
9. Let's see who can do it without looking. Close your eyes. Keep them closed.
- Everybody, point **north.** Get ready. Go. ✔
- Point **south.** Get ready. Go. ✔
- Everybody, open your eyes and stand up.
10. **(Remove N and S cards from the walls or corners.)** This is tough.
- **(Point to the S card.)**
  Everybody, point to where the letter **S** goes. ✔
- What does the letter **S** stand for? (Signal.) *South.*
- **(Point to the N card.)**
  Point to where the letter **N** goes.

- Everybody, what does the letter **N** stand for? (Signal.) *North.*
11. Wow, you are really getting smart about your directions.

Note: Save the **N** and **S** cards to post in lesson 6.

At the beginning of lesson 5 is a note to post **N** and **S** on appropriate walls or corners of the classroom. The format introduces only north and south. In lesson 8, east and west are introduced. All four directions are then reviewed in lessons 9 and 11. Here's the exercise from lesson 9.

1. Let's see how well you remember the four directions.
2. Everybody, stand up and face **north.** ✔
- Face **south.** Get ready. Go. Everybody, face north again.
3. Listen: Hold your **right** hand out to the side—straight out. Get ready. Go.
- Everybody, which direction is your right hand pointing? (Signal.) *East.* Hands down.
- Everybody, hold your **left** hand out to the side—straight out. Get ready. Go.
- Think big. Which direction is your left hand pointing? (Signal.) *West.* Hands down.
- Listen: Which direction is **behind** you? (Signal.) *South.*
  (Repeat step 3 until firm.)
4. Everybody, face **east.** East. Get ready. Go.
- Which direction are you facing? (Signal.) *East.*
- When do you see the sun in the **east?** (Signal.) *In the morning.*
5. Everybody, face **west.** Get ready. Go.
- Which direction are you facing? (Signal.) *West.*
6. Everybody, face **north.** Get ready. Go. Get ready to **point** to different directions while you keep facing **north.**

7. Listen: Everybody, point to the **west**. West. Get ready. Go.
- Point **south**. South. Get ready. Go.
- Point **east**. East. Get ready. Go.
- Point **north**. North. Get ready. Go. (Repeat step 7 until firm.)
8. I can't fool you on the four directions. Sit down.

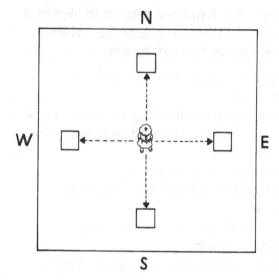

Teaching Notes

This sort of exercise should be fast and fun. All children should respond together and perform correctly. If you think that some children are "cluing" off others, direct them to close their eyes for some of the things they do. For instance, present step 3 having the children perform with their eyes closed.

If children perform poorly in part of the exercise, repeat that part. Remember, the goal of these exercises is not merely to teach skills so that children are able to perform without a great deal of effort, but to teach the skills so they are relatively easy for children. Don't accept a sloppy performance from the children. Don't be afraid to repeat parts that are weak. Reinforce children who work quickly and accurately.

In lesson 12, children are introduced to the conventions for the directions on a map. Here's the first part of the exercise from lesson 12.

- This is a map. It has the letters **N, S, E** and **W** on it. Those letters stand for **north, south, east** and **west**.
2. Everybody, touch the letter **N**. ✔ What does the **N** stand for? (Signal.) *North.*
- Listen: **North** is always at the **top** of the map.
- Everybody, touch the letter **S**. ✔ What does the **S** stand for? (Signal.) *South.*
- Listen: **South** is always at the **bottom** of the map.
- Everybody, touch the letter **E**. ✔ What does the **E** stand for? (Signal.) *East.*
- Everybody, touch the letter **W**. ✔ What does the **W** stand for? (Signal.) *West.*
3. Everybody, pick up your workbook and stand up.
- Hold your workbook flat and face north. Make the arrow for north on the map point north in the room. ✔
- Now your map shows you just which way east and west and south are.
- Look at the arrow for east on your map. It points to your right. And that's just where east is in the room.
- Look at the arrow for south. It points right through you. And that's where south is, behind you.

- Remember when the **N** on the map points north, the arrows on the map show where all the other directions are.
- Everybody, sit down.
4. Touch the person in the middle of the map. ✔
   That person wants to walk **south.** Which direction does she want to walk? **(Signal.)** *South.*
- Look at the arrows that lead from the person. Write **S** in the box on the correct arrow. That arrow shows the direction she would go to walk **south.** Raise your hand when you're finished. **(Observe children and give feedback.)**
- (Write on the board:)

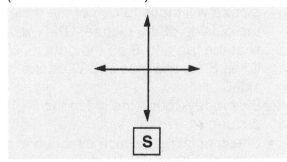

- Here's what you should have. Raise your hand if you got it right.
5. New problem: The person in the middle of the map wants to walk **east.** Which direction does she want to walk? **(Signal.)** *East.*
- Write **E** in the box on the arrow that shows which direction she would go. Raise your hand when you're finished. **(Observe children and give feedback.)**
- (Write to show:)

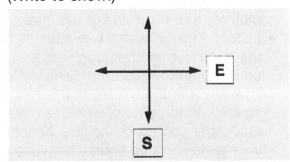

- Here's what you should have. Raise your hand if you got it right.

Teaching Notes

If the earlier work with directions in the classroom is done well, the children will have very little trouble understanding how the map works.

In step 3, children turn their map so that the directions on the map correspond to the directions in the room. This demonstration is important. It assures the children that you haven't introduced a new code for assigning the directions **north, south, east** and **west**.

Do not require children to turn their map to the north unless the exercise calls for this orientation. If you always require this orientation, children will become greatly confused with later exercises.

In lesson 15, children use instructions about **north, south, east** and **west** to solve map puzzles. Here's the first part of the exercise.

1. (Draw on the board:)

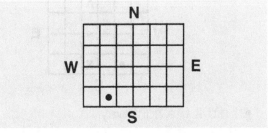

- You're going to work a puzzle. You'll have to move so many squares to the west or north or south or east.
- I'm going to move two squares to the east of the dot and put an **X** where I stop. Watch carefully.
- First I touch the dot. Then I count squares.
- **I DON'T START COUNTING UNTIL I START MOVING.**
- Listen again: I don't start counting until I start moving.

- Here I go.
  (Count:) One, two.
  (Make an **X** to show:)

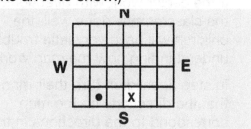

- I did it the right way.
2. Now I'll do it the wrong way. I'll say **one** when I touch the dot.
- Watch:
  (Touch the dot. Say:) One.
  (Move your finger 1 square east.
  Say:) Two.
- That's wrong because I started counting before I started moving.
3. Now I'm going to count three places north of the X I made.
- I touch the **X.** I don't start counting until I start moving.
- Here I go:
  One, two, three. (Move your finger up 3 squares north. Make an **X** to show:)

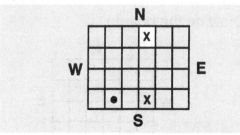

- I did it the right way.

Workbook Activity

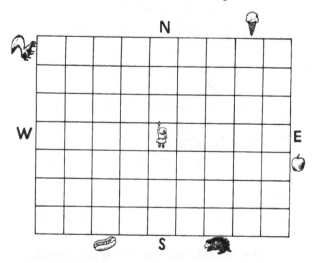

1. This is a map puzzle. The girl in the picture will move to one of the things at the outside of the picture. The map has **N** at the top and **S** on the bottom. And it has **E** on one side and **W** on the other side.
2. Everybody, touch the girl in the picture. ✔
- She is pointing. Which direction is she pointing. (Signal.) *North.*
- Tell me which direction is to her **right.** Get ready. (Signal.) *East.*
- Tell me which direction is just **behind** her. Get ready. (Signal.) *South.*
- Tell me which direction is to her **left.** Get ready. (Signal.) *West.*
3. I'll tell you how the girl moves. You'll make a little **X** with your pencil to show where she ends up. If you do it right, you'll know whether she ends up at the skunk, the hot dog or one of the other pictures at the outside of the map.
- Listen: The girl walks **two** squares to the **east.** Remember, don't start counting until you start moving. Make a little tiny **X** in the square that is two squares to the east of where she starts out. After you make the little **X,** keep your pencil on that square because that's where the girl is now.
  (Observe children and give feedback.)

4. Listen: After the girl walks two squares to the east, she walks **one** square to the north. One square to the north. Make another little **X** in the square to the north of your first **X**. Keep your pencil on the **X** that shows where the girl is now. ✔

5. Listen: Now the girl goes **four** squares to the **south**. Four squares to the south. Count the squares and make a little **X** to show where the girl ends up. Raise your hand when you know where the girl ends up. ✔

• Everybody, which picture did the girl end up at? (Signal.) *The porcupine.* I don't think she liked that very much.

Teaching Notes

The most common mistake that children make is to start counting before they start moving. (This mistake is reasonable. When children count objects, they count as soon as they touch the first object.)

As soon as you complete the board exercise and present the workbook activity, move from the front of the room and circulate among the children as you present. Make sure that children are counting appropriately and following your instructions.

Present at a reasonable pace (one that does not drag) even if some of the lower performers start to lag. If the exercise drags for children who are working at a reasonable pace, it (and similar exercises) tend to present many management problems that can be easily avoided.

In lesson 23, children are introduced to the notion of moving from one direction to another direction. Children first follow instructions for moving from one direction to another. They then work from arrows that show "to" and "from" on a map.

DIRECTIONS
Movement To/From

1. Everybody, stand up. ✔ I'm going to tell you to face different directions. Wait until I say **go.**
2. Everybody, face **north.** Get ready. Go.
• Face **west.** Get ready. Go.
• Face **south.** Get ready. Go.
• Face **north.** Get ready. Go.
• Face **east.** Get ready. Go.
3. Everybody, take two tiny steps to the **east.** Get ready. Go.
• You moved **to** the **east.** So you must have moved **from** the **west.** Everybody, which direction did you move **from**? (Signal.) *West.*
• So which direction did you move **to**? (Signal.) *East.*
4. Everybody, face **south.** Get ready. Go.
• Take two tiny steps to the **south.** Get ready. Go.
• Listen big: Which direction did you move **to**? (Signal.) *South.*
• So which direction did you move **from**? (Signal.) *North.*
5. Everybody, turn to the **north.** Take two tiny steps to the **north.** Get ready. Go.
• Listen big: Which direction did you move **to**? (Signal.) *North.*
• So which direction did you move **from**? (Signal.) *South.* Wow, you're getting pretty smart about the directions.
• Everybody, sit down.

MAP
Movement To/From

1. (Write on the board:)

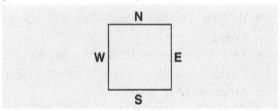

• I'm going to show you some rules about things that move.

2. (Make a dot under **N**:)

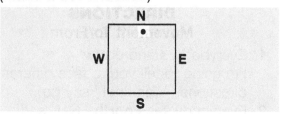

- Everybody, which side of the map is the dot on? (Signal.) *North.*
- Watch.
(Draw arrow line from dot:)

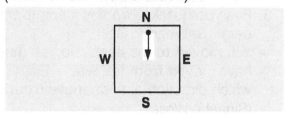

- Which direction does that line point? (Signal.) *South.*
- Yes, that line goes **from** north **to** south. Which way does that line point? (Signal.) *From north to south.*
- (Erase line and dot.)
3. (Make a dot next to **E**:)

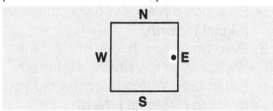

- I'm going to make another line. Watch it. (Draw line from dot:)

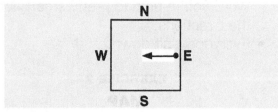

- Everybody, where did that line move **from**? (Signal.) *East.*
- Where did that line move **to**? (Signal.) *West.*
- Yes, that line went **from** east **to** west. Which way did that line move? (Signal.) *From east to west.*
- (Erase line and dot.)

4. (Make a dot next to **W**:)

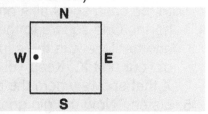

- I'm going to make another line. Watch it. (Draw a line from the dot:)

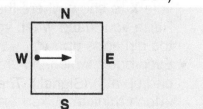

- Everybody, where did that line move **from**? (Signal.) *West.*
- Where did that line move **to**? (Signal.) *East.*
- I'm going to say the whole thing about how that line moved. The line moved from west to east.
5. Everybody, say the whole thing about how that line moved. (Signal.) *The line moved from west to east.*
(Repeat step 5 until firm.)
- (Erase line and dot.)
6. I'm going to make it harder yet. Close your eyes.
(Draw an arrow to show:)

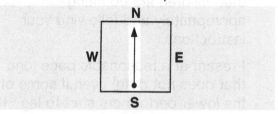

- Everybody, open your eyes. Look at this arrow. The point of the arrow shows the direction the arrow points **to.**
- Listen: Which direction does the arrow point **to**? (Signal.) *North.*
- Listen: Which direction does the arrow point **from**? (Signal.) *South.*
- Yes, the arrow points **from** south **to** north.

7. Close your eyes again.
(Change the arrow to show:)

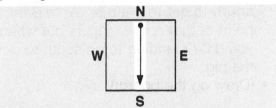

- Open your eyes. Everybody, which direction does this arrow point **to?** (Signal.) *South.*
- Which direction does it point **from?** (Signal.) *North.*
- Yes, this arrow points **from** north **to** south.

Teaching Notes

In exercise 1, keep the pacing fast. Make sure children are performing accurately. If they are, they will have very few problems relating "to" and "from" to the map.

In lessons following lesson 23, children draw routes on maps to show story events. For example, following a story about Dot and Dud, children show the route the dogs took from the kennel north to the mountain.

In lesson 33, relative direction is introduced. The scheme involves asking how you get to an object. If you go north, the object is north. If you go south, the object is south. Here's the introductory exercise.

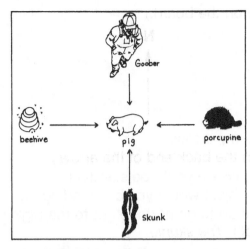

1. The pig is south of _____.
2. The pig is north of _____.
3. The pig is west of _____.
4. The pig is east of _____.

- Here's one of those tough direction games again. The arrows show how to get to the pig from different places. Remember the rule. If you have to go north to get to the pig, the pig is north. If you have to go west to get to the pig, the pig is west.
- What direction is the pig if you have to go south to get to the pig? (Signal.) *South.*
- Right, it all depends on where you are.
2. If you were standing at the back end of one of those arrows, you'd have to go **north** to get to the pig. Find the arrow that points north.
- Write **N** on the point of that arrow. ✔
- Touch the object at the back end of the arrow. That's where you'd have to be standing to go **north** to get to the pig.

- (Draw on the board:)

- Here's the arrow.
- (Touch the back end of the arrow.) Here's where you'd be standing.
- What object would you be standing on if you had to go north to get to the pig? (Signal.) *The skunk.*
- Phew. If you were standing on that skunk you'd have to go north. So the pig is north of something. What's that? (Signal.) *The skunk.*

3. Say the whole thing about the pig. (Signal.) *The pig is north of the skunk.* (Repeat step 3 until firm.)

4. If you were standing at the back end of one of these arrows, you'd have to go **east** to get to the pig. Find the arrow that points east.

- Write **E** on the point of that arrow. ✔
- Touch the object at the back end of that arrow. That's where you'd have to be standing to go east to get to the pig.
- (Draw on the board:)

- Here's the arrow.
- (Touch the back end.) Here's where you'd be standing.
- What object would you be standing on if you had to go east to get to the pig? (Signal.) *The beehive.*
- Ouch. If you were standing on that beehive, you'd have to go east to get to the pig. So the pig is east of something. What's that? (Signal.) *The beehive.*

5. Say the whole thing about the pig. (Signal.) *The pig is east of the beehive.* (Repeat step 5 until firm.)

6. If you were standing at the back end of one of those arrows, you'd have to go **south** to get to the pig. Write **S** on the point of that arrow. Figure out where you'd be standing to go south to get to the pig.

- (Draw on the board:)

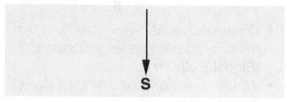

- Here's that arrow.
- (Touch the back end.) Here's where you'd be standing.
- What object would you be standing on if you had to go south to get to the pig? (Signal.) *Goober.*
- Phew. If you were standing where Goober is, you'd have to go south to get to the pig.

7. Say the whole thing about the pig. (Signal.) *The pig is south of Goober.* (Repeat step 7 until firm.)

8. If you were standing at the back of one of those arrows you'd have to go **west** to get to the pig. Write **W** on the point of that arrow. Figure out where you'd be standing to go west to get to the pig.

- (Draw on the board:)

- Here's the arrow.
- (Touch the back end.) Here's where you'd be standing.
- What object would you be standing on? (Signal.) *The porcupine.*
- Ouch. What direction would you have to go to get to the pig? (Signal.) *West.*

9. Say the whole thing about the pig. (Signal.) *The pig is west of the porcupine.* (Repeat step 9 until firm.)

Teaching Notes

Rehearse this exercise before presenting it. If you understand the basic conventions for relating what you say about the object to how you get to the object, the teaching is not greatly difficult. Make sure, however, that children are very firm in saying the statements in steps 3, 5, 7 and 9.

In later lessons, children identify where characters are on a map based on assertions that the characters make about directions. Here's an activity from lesson 46.

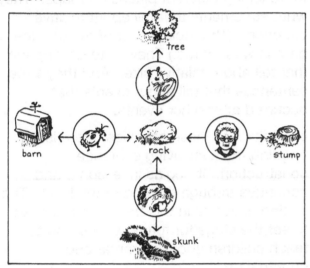

1. Bertha said, "The rock is _____ of me and the _____ is _____ of me."

2. Mrs. Hudson said, "The rock is _____ of me and the _____ is _____ of me."

3. Sherlock said, "The rock is _____ of me and the _____ is _____ of me."

1. I'll tell you what different characters said. You're going to be a detective and figure out who could have said that.
- Here's what one character said: "The rock is west of me and the stump is east of me."
- Listen again: "The rock is west of me and the stump is east of me." Raise your hand when you know who said that.

- Everybody, who said, "The rock is west of me and the stump is east of me"? (Signal.) *Mrs. Hudson.*
- Yes, Mrs. Hudson.
- Here's what another character said: "The rock is north of me and the skunk is south of me."
- Listen again: "The rock is north of me and the skunk is south of me." Raise your hand when you know who said that.
- Everybody, who said, "The rock is north of me and the skunk is south of me"? (Signal.) *Dud.*
- Yes, Dud.
- Here's what the last character said: "The rock is east of me and the barn is west of me."
- Listen again: "The rock is east of me and the barn is west of me." Raise your hand when you know who said that.
- Everybody, who said, "The rock is east of me and the barn is west of me"? (Signal.) *Bertha.*

2. You're going to complete the items. They are tough. They all start by telling about the rock. But they have a lot of blanks.
- Touch item 1. ✔
  I'll read: Bertha said, "The rock is blank of me and the blank is blank of me."
- The first part of the sentence is: The rock is blank of me. Write the word for the direction. Raise your hand when you're finished. ✔
- The first part should say: Bertha said, "The rock is **east** of me."
- Then she says that something is in another direction. Name the object that is in the other direction and write the direction. Raise your hand when you're finished. ✔
- Here's what item 1 should say: Bertha said, "The rock is east of me and the **barn** is **west** of me." Raise your hand if you got it right.

3. Touch item 2. ✔
   I'll read: Mrs. Hudson said, "The rock is blank of me and the something else is blank of me."
   - Complete the statement. Raise your hand when you're finished. ✔
   - Here's what Mrs. Hudson said: "The rock is **west** of me and the **stump** is **east** of me." Raise your hand if you got it right.
4. Touch item 3. ✔
   Sherlock said, "The rock is blank of me and the something else is blank of me."
   - Complete the statement. Raise your hand when you're finished. ✔
   - Here's what Sherlock said: "The rock is **south** of me and the **tree** is **north** of me." Raise your hand it you got it right.
   - Raise both hands if you got all those items right. I guess some of you are ready to be detectives.

Teaching Notes

This exercise presents two different skills. In the verbal exercise (step 1), children identify the character that could have made the assertion. In the writing exercise, children know who made each assertion. They fill in the blanks to complete the assertion.

To correct mistakes in the written work, tell the child who made a mistake:

1. "Touch the character."

2. "Tell how that character would move to get to the rock."
   "Go north."

3. "Say the fact about **the rock**."
   "The rock is north of the character."

4. "Tell how that character would get to the other object on the arrow." (*Student responds.*)

5. "Say the fact about that object."
   "The _____ is _____ of the character."

6. "Write the correct description."

Following the introduction of relative direction, children work on different kinds of relative-direction exercises through the end of the program. Some of these exercises relate to later stories in the program (Dooly the Duck and Dessera).

Sentence Writing and Construction

In Level B, children complete instructions for reaching different places on maps. They write statements that tell about relative direction. (The rock is east of me and the barn is west of me.) They write descriptions that tell about relative size. And they write sentences that tell about events that occurred after other events.

In addition to these activities, there is an ongoing track involving sentence construction. It begins in lesson 3 and continues through the end of the level. The writing activities in this track are designed to set the stage for future writing and to teach children about grammar and punctuation.

All sentence–construction activities present sentences that are of the form: subject–predicate. The reason is that sentences of this form are the most informative about both punctuation and grammar. More complicated sentences are often transformations of basic sentences. (A sentence such as, "After school, we went home," is a transformation of the subject–predicate sentence, "We went home after school.")

In Level B, children learn the basic sentence–construction rule of naming and then telling more. In the initial exercises, they refer to a picture that shows a familiar character doing something. They name the character and tell what the character did. This procedure was introduced in Level A.

Here's an early sentence-construction activity from lesson 7 of Level B.

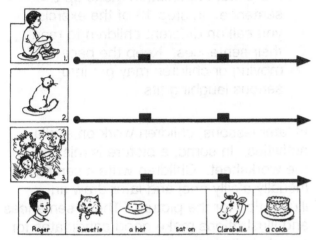

The pictures show what different characters did. You're going to write sentences that tell what the characters did in each picture.

2. Look at the boxes below the arrows. There are words at the bottom of each box. I'll read the words.
   • Touch the first box.
     The word says: **Roger.**
   • Touch the next box.
     The word says: **Sweetie.**
   • Touch the next box.
     The words say: **a hat.**
   • Touch the next box.
     There's no picture.
     The words say: **sat on.**
   • Touch the next box.
     The word says: **Clarabelle.**
   • Touch the last box.
     The words say: **a cake.**

3. Everybody, touch picture 1. ✔
   Who's in that picture? (Signal.) *Roger.*
   • What did Roger do in this picture?
     (Call on a child. Idea: *Sat on a hat.*)
   • Here's the sentence that tells what Roger did: **Roger sat on a hat.**
4. Everybody, say that sentence.
   (Signal.) *Roger sat on a hat.*
   (Repeat step 4 until firm.)
5. For each space on the arrow, you'll write the words that are in one of the boxes below the arrows.
6. Touch the first space on the arrow for picture 1. ✔
   What will you write in that space?
   (Signal.) *Roger.*
   • Touch the middle space. ✔
     What will you write in that space?
     (Signal.) *Sat on.*
   • Touch the last space. ✔
     What will you write in that space?
     (Signal.) *A hat.*
     (Repeat step 6 until firm.)
7. Your turn: Write sentence 1.
   Remember to spell the words correctly. Start with a capital letter and end with a period. Raise your hand when you're finished.
   (Observe children and give feedback.)
   • (Write on the board:)

   Roger ▮ **sat on** ▮ **a hat.** ➤

   • Here's what you should have for sentence 1.
     Raise your hand if you got it right.

8. Touch picture 2. ✔
   Now you're going to make up a
   sentence for picture 2. That picture
   shows what another character did.
   - Who's in that picture? (Signal.)
     Sweetie.
   - Raise your hand if you can say the
     whole sentence about what Sweetie did
     in picture 2. Remember to use words
     from the boxes below the arrows.
     (Call on a child.) *Sweetie sat on a hat.*
   - Yes, Sweetie sat on a hat.
9. Everybody, say that sentence. (Signal.)
   Sweetie sat on a hat.
   (Repeat step 9 until firm.)
10. Your turn: Write the sentence on the
    arrow for picture 2. Write the words
    Sweetie, sat on, a hat. Copy the words
    carefully. Start with a capital letter and
    end with a period. Raise your hand
    when you're finished.
    (Observe children and give feedback.)
11. Touch picture 3. ✔
    Uh-oh, it's hard to tell what's in that
    picture. In fact, maybe there's not even
    a hat in that picture. Maybe there's a
    cake, and maybe somebody sat on
    that cake.
12. Your turn: Write sentence 3. Start with
    the name of somebody. Then tell what
    that character sat on. Don't write one
    of the sentences you've already written.
    Raise your hand when you're finished.
    (Observe children and give feedback.)
13. Read the sentence you wrote for
    picture 3. (Call on several children.
    Praise sentences of the form _____ sat
    on _____.)
    - We have some pretty silly sentences.
14. Raise your hand if all your sentences
    start with a capital and end with a
    period.
    - Let's see who can read all three of their
      sentences. (Call on several children.
      Praise correct responses.)

Teaching Notes

The pictures form the basis for the
sentences. In the early exercises,
the pictures are carefully controlled
so that children will succeed in their
early writing endeavors. This feature
is very important.

For picture 3, children make up a
sentence. In step 13 of the exercise,
you call on different children to read
their sentences. Keep the pace
moving or children may get into
serious laughing fits.

In later lessons, children work on similar
activities. In some, a picture is missing on
the worksheet. Children write a sentence
(usually a silly one) and later draw an
illustration for the picture. These sentences
and illustrations make good candidates for
a lively bulletin board.

In lessons 21, 26 and 31, children compose
simple stories based on a common theme
or action. These stories follow a form of
going from general to specific. The first
sentence tells what everybody did. The
following sentences tell what individual
characters did. The pattern that is used is
common in both poems and simple
elaborations (main idea followed by detail).

The lessons in which these writing activities
are presented differ from other lessons in
Level B. The writing is the only activity
presented in these lessons.

To compose their sentences, children refer to the illustrations and names on their workbook page. Here's the first part of the work in lesson 21.

1.

———————————————
———————————————
———————————————
———————————————

2.

———————————————
———————————————
———————————————
———————————————

3.

———————————————
———————————————
———————————————
———————————————

a hot dog | a chicken | a bike | a horse | a toad | a pot
a note | a mouse | a paddle | an apple | a cow | a ladder
a tub | a book | a chair | an ant | a bottle | a barn
a dime | a house | a puppy | a cup | a plum | a door

- Today's lesson is different. You're going to write sentences. Then you're going to draw pictures for **two** of your favorite sentences.
2. Touch number 1. ✔
   You're going to write your first sentence on the top line.
- (Write on the board:)

Everybody found something.

- This says: Everybody found something.
- Copy that sentence on the top line of number 1. Remember the capital and the period. Raise your hand when you've copied the sentence.
  (Observe children and give feedback.)

3. On the next line you'll tell what **Goober** found. He found one of the things that you see at the bottom of the page. There are lots of things on that page. Maybe he found a puppy. Maybe he found that tub.
- Name something else he might have found. **(Call on different children.)**
- (Write to show:)

Everybody found something.
Goober found _____.

- Here's the first part of the sentence. Write the sentence for Goober. Remember to spell the words just the way they are shown in the picture. Raise your hand when you've finished. Remember to start with a capital and end with a period.
  (Observe children and give feedback.)
- (Call on different children to read their sentence for Goober. Praise acceptable sentences.)
4. (Write to show:)

Everybody found something.
Goober found _____.
Liz _____.
I _____.

- On the next line you'll write what **Liz** found.
- On the bottom line you'll write what **you** found.
- Remember, each sentence starts with a capital and ends with a period. Raise your hand when you've written a sentence for Liz and a sentence for you.
  (Observe children and give feedback.)
- (Call on different children to read their sentence about Liz. Then call on different children to read their sentence about themselves. Praise acceptable sentences.)
5. Touch number 2. ✔
   The sentences you'll write for number 2 tell what different characters **painted.**

- (Write on the board:)

  Everybody painted something

- This says: Everybody painted something.
- Copy that sentence on the top line of number 2. Remember the capital and period. Raise your hand when you're finished.
  (Observe children and give feedback.)
6. (Write to show:)

  Everybody painted something.
  Roger painted _____.

- On the next line you'll tell what **Roger** painted. He painted one of the things that you see at the bottom of the page. Maybe he painted a ladder. Maybe he painted a tub.
- Write your sentence for Roger. Raise your hand when you're finished.
  (Observe children and give feedback.)
- (Call on different children to read their sentence for Roger. Praise acceptable sentences.)
7. (Write to show:)

  Everybody painted something.
  Roger painted _____.
  Molly _____.
  I _____.

- On the next line you'll write what **Molly** painted.
- On the bottom line you'll write what **you** painted.

- Don't forget the capital and period for each sentence. Raise your hand when you've written a sentence for Molly and a sentence for you.
  (Observe children and give feedback.)
- (Call on different children to read their sentence about Molly. Then call on different children to read their sentence about themselves. Praise acceptable sentences.)

Optional story-writing activities are presented in lessons 34, 37, 43 and 46. The optional activities follow the same basic format as the exercise from lesson 21, except that students refer to their workbook page titled Story words. Here's the optional activity at the end of lesson 37.

Story words

Sentence Writing

Note: This is an optional writing activity to be presented before lesson 38. For this activity children will need lined paper. Pass out paper. Direct children to write their name on the top line.

1. Everybody, find the page titled **Story words** at the front of your workbook.
- Today, you're going to write sentences that make up little stories.

2. (Write on the board:)

> **Everybody played.**

- This says: Everybody played.
- Copy that sentence on the second line of your paper. Remember the capital and the period. Raise your hand when you've copied the sentence.
(Observe children and give feedback.)

3. (Write to show:)

> **Everybody played.**
> **Dot played with _____.**

- Here's the first part of the sentence you'll write next. Dot played with blank. You're going to complete the sentence for Dot. She played with one of the things shown on the page with **Story words.**
- Write your sentence about Dot. Raise your hand when you're finished.
(Observe children and give feedback.)
- (Call on different children to read their sentence for Dot.)

4. (Write to show:)

> **Everybody played.**
> **Dot played with _____.**
> **Zelda _____.**
> **I _____.**

- You're going to write more sentences. One will tell about Zelda and what she played with. The other will tell about you and what you played with.
- Your turn: Write both sentences. Remember the period at the end of each sentence. Raise your hand when you're finished.
(Observe children and give feedback.)
- (Call on different children to read their sentence about Zelda. Then call on different children to read their sentence about themselves.)

Teaching Notes

These activities take time because children write slowly; however, the activities provide children with important practice. If time permits, optional activities can be presented later during the day or even during the period slated for the next language lesson.

Although the program provides structured directions for presenting optional activities in only three lessons, it is possible to present them more frequently and to expand what children do. Be careful with expansions, however. As a simple guide, make sure that students write sentences that first name and then tell more (what the character did, what the character had, or what the character was). Keep the writing in the past tense.

REPORTING

Starting in lesson 56, children learn about sentences that report. The rule is that a sentence reports on a picture if you can touch something in the picture that shows what the sentence says. Here's the exercise from lesson 57. Children indicate whether sentences report by circling the words **reports** or **does not report.**

A.

1. Sherlock ate too much corn.	reports	does not report
2. Bertha was mad at Sherlock.	reports	does not report
3. Cyrus pulled a large sack.	reports	does not report
4. Bertha played a violin.	reports	does not report
5. The wise old rat was dirty.	reports	does not report
6. The sack was full of hazelnuts.	reports	does not report
7. The wise old rat was wet.	reports	does not report

1. Look at the picture in part A. Remember, if a sentence tells about something that you can touch in the picture, the sentence **reports** on the picture. If the sentence does not tell about something you can touch, the sentence **does not report.**

2. Listen: Bertha played a violin. That sentence reports. Touch the part of the picture that shows: Bertha played a violin. ✔
   - Listen: Cyrus was mad at Sherlock. Everybody, does that sentence report? (Signal.) *No.*
   - Right, nothing in the picture shows: Cyrus was mad at Sherlock.

3. Listen: The sack that Cyrus was pulling belonged to Sherlock. Everybody, does that sentence report? (Signal.) *No.*
   - The picture doesn't show who the sack belongs to.
   - Listen: Two rats were sitting. Everybody, does that sentence report? (Signal.) *Yes.*
   - Touch the part of the picture that shows: Two rats were sitting. ✔
   - Listen: The wise old rat was taking a shower. Everybody, does that sentence report? (Signal.) *Yes.*
   - Listen: Bertha was playing a pretty tune. Everybody, does that sentence report? (Signal.) *No.*
   - It doesn't report because the picture doesn't show the music is a pretty tune. Maybe she's just making squeaking sounds.

4. Everybody, touch sentence 1 below the picture. Sentence 1.
   I'll read sentence 1: Sherlock ate too much corn. Everybody, does that sentence report? (Signal.) *No.*
   - The sentence does not report, so circle the words does not report. Find the words **does not report** on the same line as sentence 1 and circle them.

5. Everybody, touch sentence 2.
   I'll read sentence 2: Bertha was mad at Sherlock. Everybody, does that sentence report? (Signal.) *No.*
   - The sentence does not report, so circle the words **does not report** on the same line as sentence 2.

6. I'll read the rest of the sentences. Touch each sentence as I read it. Don't circle anything. Just touch the sentences.
   - Sentence 3: Cyrus pulled a large sack.
   - Sentence 4: Bertha played a violin.
   - Sentence 5: The wise old rat was dirty.
   - Sentence 6: The sack was full of hazelnuts.
   - Sentence 7: The wise old rat was wet.

7. Your turn: Circle the right words for the sentences. Read each sentence to yourself. If the sentence reports, circle **reports.** If the sentence does not report, circle **does not report.** Raise your hand when you're finished. (Observe children and give feedback.)

8. Let's check your work. Look at the picture. Make an **X** next to any item you missed. I'll read each sentence. You tell me whether you circled **reports** or **does not report.**
- Sentence 3: Cyrus pulled a large sack. What did you circle? (Signal.) *Reports.*
- Sentence 4: Bertha played a violin. What did you circle? (Signal.) *Reports.*
- Sentence 5: The wise old rat was dirty. What did you circle? (Signal.) *Does not report.*
- Sentence 6: The sack was full of hazelnuts. What did you circle? (Signal.) *Does not report.*
- Sentence 7: The wise old rat was wet. What did you circle? (Signal.) *Reports.*

9. Raise your hand if you got no items wrong. Great job.
- Raise your hand if you got only 1 item wrong. Good work.
- Listen: Fix up any mistakes you made in part A. Do it now. Circle the right words for any items you missed. (Observe children and give feedback.)

Teaching Note
When presenting steps 6, 7 and 8, circulate among the children. Allow children a reasonable amount of time to complete the work in step 7. In step 8, make sure they are correcting any mistakes.

Starting in lesson 57, children construct sentences that **report.** These sentences tell the main thing that a character did. Here's the activity from lesson 58.

| washed | mopped | read | painted | book |
| window | floor | piano | | |

(Pass out lined paper.)
- You're going to write sentences that report on the main thing that each character did in this picture. Each sentence you'll write will name the character and then tell what the character did.

2. Touch Bleep. ✔
- Raise your hand when you know the main thing Bleep did.
- Everybody, what did Bleep do? (Signal.) *Mopped the floor.*
- Here's the whole sentence for Bleep: Bleep mopped the floor. Everybody, say that sentence. (Signal.) *Bleep mopped the floor.*

3. Touch Molly. ✔ Raise your hand when you can say the whole sentence that tells what Molly did. Remember, start with Molly and tell what she **did.**
- (Call on a child.) Say the sentence for Molly. (Idea: *Molly washed the window.*)
- Here's the sentence for Molly: Molly washed the window. Everybody, say that sentence. (Signal.) *Molly washed the window.*

4. Touch Paul. ✔
- Raise your hand when you can say the whole sentence that tells what Paul did.
- (Call on a child.) Say the sentence for Paul. (Idea: *Paul painted a piano.*)
- Here's the sentence for Paul: Paul painted a piano. Everybody, say that sentence. (Signal.) *Paul painted a piano.*
5. Touch Zelda. ✔
- Raise your hand when you can say the whole sentence that tells what Zelda did.
- (Call on a child.) Say the sentence for Zelda. (Idea: *Zelda read a book.*)
- I wonder if she's reading Mrs. Hudson's book.
- Here's the sentence for Zelda: Zelda read a book. Everybody, say that sentence. (Signal.) *Zelda read a book.*
6. Touch the vocabulary box. That's the box with the words in it. These are words that you will use when you write your sentences. I'll read the words: washed . . . mopped . . . read (red) . . . painted . . . book . . . window . . . floor . . . piano.
7. Your turn: Write your sentence for Bleep. Start your sentence with Bleep. Tell what he did. Remember to spell the words correctly and end your sentence with a period. Raise your hand when you're finished.
(Observe children and give feedback.)
- (Write on the board:)

Bleep mopped the floor.

- Here's what you should have for your sentence that reports on Bleep.

8. Your next sentence will report on the main thing Molly did. Remember, start with Molly. Tell the main thing she did. Raise your hand when you're finished. (Observe children and give feedback.)
- (Write on the board:)

Molly washed the window.

- Here's what you should have for Molly.
9. Your next sentence will report on the main thing Paul did. Start with Paul and tell the main thing he did. Raise your hand when you're finished.
(Observe children and give feedback.)
- (Write on the board:)

Paul painted a piano.

- Here's what you should have for Paul.
10. Your next sentence will report on the main thing Zelda did. Start with Zelda and tell the main thing she did. Raise your hand when you're finished.
(Observe children and give feedback.)
- (Write on the board:)

Zelda read a book.

- Here's what you should have for Zelda.
11. Raise your hand if you got all the sentences right. Good for you.
- Later you can color the picture. I wonder what color Paul painted the piano.

INFERENCE

For the last type of writing activity presented in Level B, children write sentences that infer what must have happened in a picture that is missing.

Two pictures are shown. Between them is a blank picture. Some things that occurred in the blank picture can be inferred by referring to the first and last pictures. Any difference in these pictures implies something that must have happened in the middle picture.

Inferences are introduced in lesson 66.
Here's the activity from lesson 67.

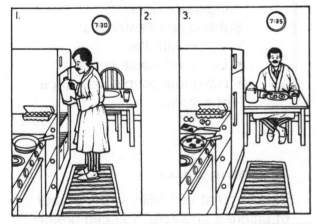

eggs	cooked	poured	took	bottle
refrigerator	breakfast	plate	table	
glass	cracked	milk	carton	closed

This is another mystery picture. Remember, the first picture shows where the man was first and what he did first.

- It's morning in the first picture. The clock shows that it's 7:30.
- The mystery picture is next. It's supposed to show what the man did just after he did the things in the first picture.
- The last picture shows what he did just after doing the things in the mystery picture. That picture shows that it's now 7:35 in the morning.
2. Remember how to figure out what happened in the mystery picture. You look at the first picture and the last picture. You ask yourself what's different in the last picture. Anything that's different in the last picture gives a clue about something that must have happened in the mystery picture.
- In the first picture, the man is standing by the refrigerator. Everybody, is he by the refrigerator in the last picture? (Signal.) *No.*
- That gives a clue about one thing he must have done in the mystery picture.

- Everybody, look at the eggs in the first picture. They're in a carton. Everybody, are they all in a carton in the last picture? (Signal.) *No.*
- That gives you more clues about what the man did in the mystery picture.
- Look at the plate in the first picture. What's on that plate? (Signal.) *Nothing.*
- What's on the plate in the last picture? (Signal.) *Two eggs.*
- That gives you more clues about the mystery picture.
3. Touch the words in the vocabulary box. I'll read them. Follow along: eggs . . . cooked . . . poured . . . took . . . bottle . . . refrigerator . . . breakfast . . . plate . . . table . . . glass . . . cracked . . . milk . . . carton. . .closed.
4. (Write on the board:)

The man

- The first sentence you'll write about the mystery picture will tell the thing the man did first in the mystery picture. That sentence starts with **the man.**
- Listen: On your lined paper, write the first sentence. Start with the words **the man** and tell the first thing he did. Remember, just one sentence. That sentence should tell what the man did just after the first picture. Think of the first thing he must have done and write the sentence. Raise your hand when you're finished.
(Observe children and give feedback.)
- (Write to show:)

The man close the refrigerator door.

- Here's a good first sentence. Raise your hand if you wrote a sentence like that. (Call on different children:) Read your sentence.
(Praise sentences that express the idea that the man closed the refrigerator door.)

5. (Write below:)

He

- The rest of your sentences will begin with the word **he** and will tell other things the man did. Each sentence should tell about one thing he did. And the sentences should be in a good order. I hope nobody has the man eat those eggs before they are cooked.
- You can write as many sentences as you want. Remember, any difference between the first picture and the last picture gives a clue about something that happened. Tell about the things the man must have done. Write your sentences. Raise your hand when you're finished.
  (Observe children and give feedback.)
6. I'll read a good description of what must have happened in the mystery picture:
   The man closed the refrigerator door.
   He poured a glass of milk.
   He put the bottle of milk on the table.
   He cooked some eggs.
   He put the eggs on his plate.
   He sat down.
- That's a lot of sentences.
7. I'll call on different children to read what they wrote. I'll act out the things each sentence says. We'll see if the description makes sense or if I have to eat eggs that I forgot to put on my plate or forgot to cook.
- (Call on different children:) Read your first sentence. (Act it out.)
  Read your next sentence. (Act it out.)
- (After each description has been read, ask:) Is that a good description of what must have happened in the mystery picture?
- (Praise good descriptions.)

Key: First sentence begins with **The man** and tells that he closed the refrigerator door.
Subsequent sentences:
- Begin with **he**.
- Use past-tense verbs.
- Have reasonable sequence of events.

Teaching Notes

Expect great variability in the output of different children. You can greatly increase the output of some by challenging them. "I know that some of you are going to write only a couple of sentences. Others are going to write a lot. That's great when you write a lot. Raise your hand if you're going to write a lot."

When observing the children, make frequent announcements about who is writing a lot. "Some people have already written four sentences. And they are good sentences."

When you call on children to read what they have written (step 7), praise children who have written at least four sentences.

If the group's work is sloppy, repeat the exercise as part of the next lesson. If possible, present a reinforcer for children who write at least four good sentences.

Spatial Orientation

Level B provides a lot of work with diagrams that imply movement. These activities address a need that children have to interpret diagrams and illustrations. To view an action picture appropriately is to consider what is shown with respect to what happened just before the picture and what will happen after the picture. Children who have this understanding have a great advantage in understanding much of what is illustrated in science and social studies texts, as well as what is illustrated in their reading textbooks.

The work with spatial orientation begins in lesson 16 and continues to the end of the level.

ROUTES

The first spatial orientation activities involve tracing a route and identifying the objects that are facing the wrong direction. The object of these exercises is to establish procedures for converting a static picture into an operation. By starting at the beginning of the route shown in the picture and following it, children can identify the objects that are facing the wrong direction. Here's the exercise from lesson 17, the second lesson involving continuous movement.

This path shows the route the rat took when he practiced for a race. The path starts with rat 1 and goes to rat 10.
• Touch the rat at 1. He's near the top of the picture. ✔

• There are some mistakes again. There are **three** rats that are facing the wrong direction. It's hard to see which rats those are unless you start with rat 1 and follow the path the rat took.
2. Your turn: Start at rat 1. Then follow the path the rat took and see if you can find all three rats that are facing the wrong direction. Cross out the **three** rats that are facing the wrong way. Remember to follow the path or you'll get fooled just like the people who made this picture. Raise your hand when you're finished.
(Observe children and give feedback.)
3. Check your work.
• Everybody, start at the beginning of the path and move your finger to the first rat that's facing the wrong direction. ✔
• What's the number of the first rat that is wrong? (Signal.) *Six.*
• Yes, so you should have crossed out rat 6.
4. Now go to the next rat that is facing the wrong direction. ✔
• Everybody, what's the number of the next rat that's facing the wrong direction? (Signal.) *Nine.*
• Yes, so you should have crossed out rat 9.
5. Now go to the last rat that's facing the wrong direction. ✔
• Everybody, what's the number of the last rat that's facing the wrong direction? (Signal.) *Ten.*
• Yes, so you should have crossed out rat 10.
6. Raise your hand if you crossed out all three rats that are wrong.
Good for you.

In the next lesson (lesson 18), children do a similar activity with a different route. For this exercise, however, children cut out the rats and place them at specified points on the route.

CONNECTED COMPONENTS

In lesson 19, children draw arrows to show the movement of a rope. Here's the exercise.

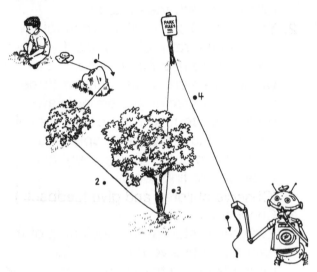

1. (Draw on the board:)

- You're going to draw arrows that show the way something is moving. These balls show the starting point for the arrows. For the first ball, I'll draw an arrow that shows something moving straight up.
- I start at the ball to draw the arrow. Watch.
  (Add to show:)

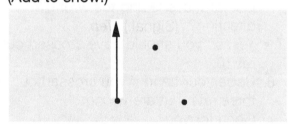

- For the next ball, I'll draw the arrow for something moving straight to the right.
- Point and show me the direction the arrow will point. (Children point right.)
- I start at the ball and draw the arrow. Watch.

(Add to show:)

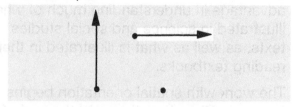

- The last ball will show something moving **down** and to the **left.** Down and to the left. Point and show me which way the arrow will point.
  (Children point down and to the left.)
- (Add to show:)

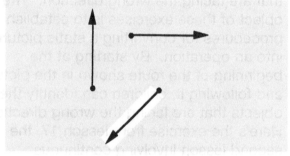

2. Everybody, find part B.
   This is a picture that shows somebody playing a trick on Roger. Somebody tied a string to Roger's hat. That somebody is going to pull on the string and make Roger's hat move.
3. Who's pulling the hat? (Signal.) *Bleep.*
   Yes, it's Bleep playing a joke on Roger.
4. Touch the arrow by Bleep's hand. ✔
   The arrow shows the direction Bleep is moving one end of the string. When Bleep moves the string in that direction, the whole string will move in that direction and Roger's hat will move, too.
5. Touch number 1 by Roger's hat. ✔
   The arrow at number 1 shows where Roger's hat will go first.
6. Touch number 2. ✔
   There's no arrow at number 2, just a little ball.
- Listen: Figure out the path that Roger's hat will take and draw the arrow for number 2. Start at the ball and draw the arrow that shows the direction his hat will be moving at number 2. Raise your hand when you're finished.
  (Observe children and give feedback.)

- (Draw on the board:)

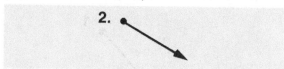

- Here's the arrow you should have at number 2. Raise your hand if you got it right.
7. Listen: Follow the path that Roger's hat will take and draw the arrow for number 3. Start at the ball and show the direction his hat will be moving at number 3. Raise your hand when you're finished.
   (Observe children and give feedback.)
- (Draw on the board:)

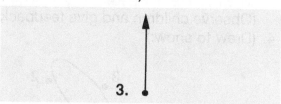

- Here's the arrow you should have at number 3. Raise your hand if you got it right.
8. Listen: Follow the path that Roger's hat will take and draw the arrow for number 4. Show the direction his hat will be moving at number 4.
   Raise your hand when you're finished.
   (Observe children and give feedback.)
- (Draw on the board:)

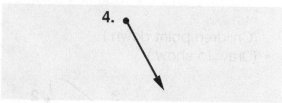

- Here's the arrow you should have at number 4.
- Raise your hand if you got it right.

9. I wonder what Roger will think when he sees his hat moving around rocks and bushes that way.

Teaching Note

The biggest problem that children have with drawing arrows is relating the arrow to the ball. Sometimes, they make the point at the ball and then become confused. The prompt that you should provide if they have trouble is: "Touch the ball. Now move in the direction that the string is moving. Now do the same thing with your pencil. Touch the ball. Move in the direction the string is moving. Now make the tip of the arrow."

Variations of arrow-drawing are presented in different lessons. For some lessons, the orientation exercise relates to different topics children study. For instance, lesson 33 presents a story in which an injured mountain climber is rescued. To lower the climber down a steep slope, the ranger drives a stake in the snow, attaches a rope to the climber's sled and lowers the sled from below. Here's the exercise from lesson 33.

This picture shows a ranger lowering an injured mountain climber down a very steep slope. At the top of the slope is a great stake that's stuck way down in the snow so it won't slip.

- Everybody, touch the stake at the top of the slope. ✔
  There's a rope that goes around the stake. The ranger is holding onto one end of the rope. The other end is attached to a sled basket that's holding the injured mountain climber.
- Everybody, touch the sled basket. ✔
  There's a big dot next to that sled basket and a number 1.
- Touch the dot for number 1. ✔
2. You're going to draw an arrow next to the sled basket to show the direction it will move. Remember, the ranger is **lowering** the injured mountain climber. That basket will move down the slope. Draw the arrow next to the sled basket. Raise your hand when you're finished.
  (Observe children and give feedback.)

- (Draw on the board:)

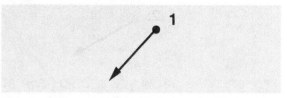

- Here's the direction your arrow should be pointing. Raise your hand if you got it right. ✔
3. Listen: Along the rope are more dots that show which way the rope will move. On each dot, draw an arrow to show which way the rope will move. Start with dot 2. Be careful and don't make any silly arrows. Raise your hand when you're finished.
  (Observe children and give feedback.)
4. (Draw to show:)

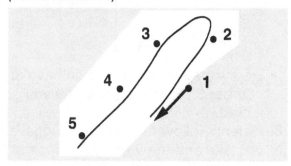

- Here's a picture of the rope with the 5 dots on it.
5. Look at number 2.
- Everybody, use your finger and point to show the way the rope is moving at number 2.
  (Children point down.)
- (Draw to show:)

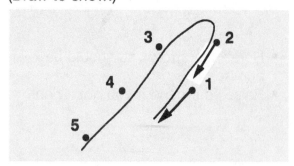

- Here's the arrow for 2.
- Look at number 3. Everybody, point to show the way the rope is moving at number 3.
  (Children point up.)

- (Draw to show:)

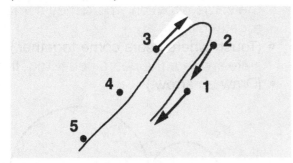

- Here's the arrow for 3.
- Look at number 4. Everybody, point to show the way the rope is moving at number 4.
  (Children point up.)
- (Draw to show:)

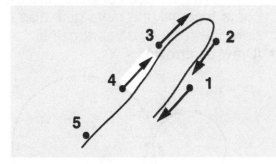

- Here's the arrow for 4.
- Look at number 5. Everybody, point to show the way the rope is moving at number 5.
  (Children point up.)
- (Draw to show:)

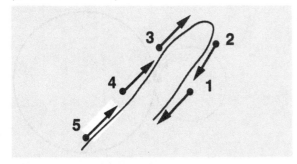

- Here's the arrow for 5.
6. Raise your hand if you got all the arrows right. ✔
- Good work.
7. Later you can color the picture.

In lessons 37 and 38, children apply what they have learned about continuous movement to identifying how power is transmitted to the rear wheel in a bicycle power train. Here's the exercise from lesson 38.

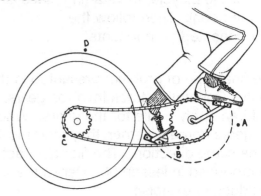

1. This is one of those drawings that shows how a bicycle works. You'll have to draw arrows at each letter.
- Touch A.
  You'll have to draw an arrow to show which direction that pedal will move.
- Touch B.
  You'll have to draw the arrow at B. Remember, the chain moves the same way the pedal moves. So figure out which way the pedal moves, and you'll know the direction of the arrow at B.
- Then complete the arrows at C and D. Do not make a silly mistake. Remember, you want that bike to go forward, not backward. Raise your hand when you're finished.
  (Observe children and give feedback.)
2. (Draw on the board:)

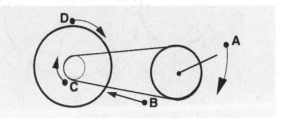

- Here's what you should have for each letter.
- Raise your hand if you got everything right.

Teaching Note

The procedure for tracing the route in all these exercises is the same. Start where the system is acted on. For the bicycle, the starting place is the pedal. Then follow the connected components.

The final type of problem presented in the Spatial Orientation track involves gears. Children apply a rule for the gears. Where the gears come together, they start moving in the same direction. The first gear activity is introduced in lesson 58. Here's the introductory exercise.

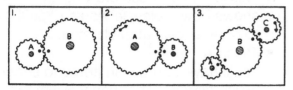

1. Touch picture 1. ✔
• That picture shows two gears. Gears are just like wheels that turn together. They turn together because the gear teeth are joined.
• Touch where the two gears come together.
   (Observe children and give feedback.)
• (Draw on the board:)

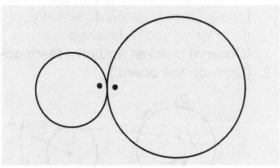

• Here are the two gears without the gear teeth. I'll tell you the rule about gears. Listen: The gears always start **in the same direction** where they come together.

• Listen again: The gears always start in the same direction where they come together.
• (Touch where gears come together.) Here's where the gears come together.
• (Draw an arrow:)

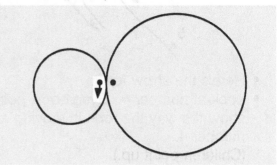

• So, if this gear goes down where they come together, the other gear also goes down where they come together.
• (Draw an arrow:)

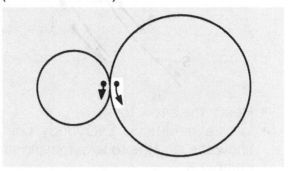

2. Here's another problem. (Change arrows to show:)

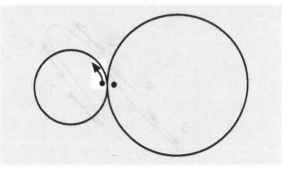

• If one gear goes **up** where they come together, which way does the other gear move? (Signal.) *Up.*

- (Draw an arrow:)

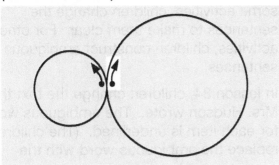

3. Your turn to draw arrows for the gears in picture 1. Listen: Gear A is going down where they come together. Draw the arrows for both gears in picture 1. Raise your hand when you're finished.
- (Draw on the board:)

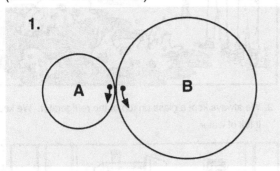

- Here's what you should have.
4. Touch picture 2. ✔
- This is tricky. There's one arrow showing which way gear A is turning. But that arrow is not on the side where the gears are coming together.
- Your turn: Draw the arrow for the other dot on gear A. Then draw the arrow on gear B. Raise your hand when you're finished.

  (Observe children and give feedback.)
- (Draw on the board:)

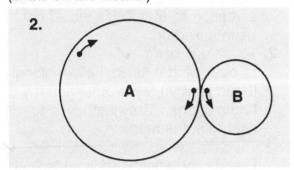

- Here's what you should have for picture 2.

5. Touch picture 3. ✔

This is a very tricky picture. There are three gears. There's one arrow on gear C. But there are no other arrows on the other gears. Remember the rule: The gears start in the same direction where they come together.
- Draw the arrows where gears C and B come together. Raise your hand when you're finished.
- (Draw on the board:)

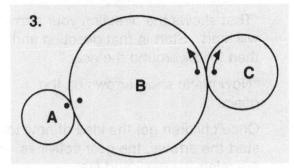

- Here's what you should have so far.
6. Now draw the arrow for the other side of gear B. Then draw the arrow for gear A. Raise your hand when you're finished.
- (Draw on the board:)

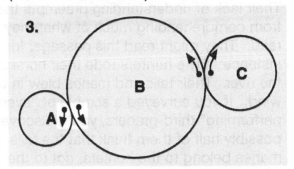

- Here's what you should have. These gears are pretty tricky, aren't they?

Teaching Note

To correct children who have trouble with the gears, tell them:

"Touch where the gears come together. Touch with one finger."

"Both the gears start moving in the same direction where your finger is. Start moving your finger in that direction. Just move it a little bit."

"That shows the direction your arrow will start. Start in that direction and then follow around the gear."

"Now make short arrows on the gears."

Once children get the idea of how to start the arrows, the gear activities are relatively easy and fast.

Clarity

Children entering the third grade often do not have a clear sense of pronoun referents. Their lack of understanding preempts them from comprehending much of what they read. They might read this passage, for instance: "The hunters rode their horses to the river. Their tails and manes blew in the wind." If you surveyed a sample of "average performing" third-graders, you'd discover possibly half of them think that the tails and manes belong to the hunters, not to the horses. These children will have serious comprehension problems when reading much of what they are expected to understand.

Understanding the use of pronouns is important also for writing clearly. Level B presents many exercises involving pronoun clarity, starting at lesson 34 and continuing to the end of the level. The context for most of the exercises involves pictures.

Sentences are compared with pictures. For some activities, children change the sentences to make them clear. For other activities, children construct ambiguous sentences.

In lesson 34, children change the text that Mrs. Hudson wrote. The ambiguous word for each item is underlined. (The children replace the ambiguous word with the correct name.)

1. My brother and my sister had pet pigs. They just loved to roll around in the mud.

2. We always kept a glass on top of the refrigerator. We kept it full of water.

Those are the sentences that Mrs. Hudson circled. The pictures show what she **wanted** Zelda's pictures to show. Mrs. Hudson could have changed the underlined part of each sentence so that Zelda would not have been mixed up.

2. Touch number **1.** ✔
   I'll read what it says. Follow along:
* (Read slowly:) My brother and my sister had pet pigs. They just loved to roll around in the mud.
* Touch the word that's underlined. ✔ Everybody, what word is underlined? (Signal.) *They.*

- Yes, **they. They** just loved to roll around in the mud.
- If Mrs. Hudson changed the word **they** to the right name, Zelda wouldn't have been confused. Everybody, what's the right name? **(Signal.)** *The pigs.*
- Listen: Cross out the word **they** and write **the pigs.** Raise your hand when you're finished.
(Observe children and give feedback.)
- Now it says: My brother and my sister had pet pigs. **The pigs** just loved to roll around in the mud.
3. Touch number 2. ✔
I'll read what it says. Follow along:
- **(Read slowly:)** We always kept a glass on top of the refrigerator. We kept it full of water.
- Touch the word that's underlined. ✔
Everybody, what word is underlined? **(Signal.)** *It.*
- Yes, **it.** We kept **it** full of water.
- If Mrs. Hudson changed the word **it** to the right name, Zelda wouldn't have been confused. Everybody, what's the right name? **(Signal.)** *The glass.*
- Cross out the word **it** and write **the glass** above the crossed-out **it.** Raise your hand when you're finished.
(Observe children and give feedback.)
- Now it says: We always kept a glass on top of the refrigerator. We kept **the glass** full of water. Now that's clear and Zelda would not be confused.
- Later you can color the pictures.

In lesson 35, children work with the same pair of items, but they indicate what Zelda (the confused artist) thought Mrs. Hudson wanted. (The children replace the ambiguous word with the unintended name.)

1. My brother and my sister had pet pigs. <u>They</u> just loved to roll around in the mud.

2. We always kept a glass on top of the refrigerator. We kept <u>it</u> full of water.

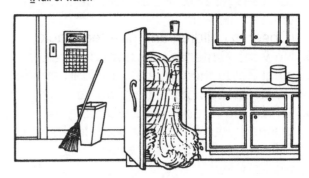

These are the illustrations that Zelda drew for two parts of the story.
- You're going to fix up the sentences with the names that Zelda thought the sentences were talking about.
2. Touch number 1. ✔
The picture below number 1 shows Mrs. Hudson's brother and sister rolling around in the mud.
- I'll read what number 1 says. You follow along: My brother and my sister had pet pigs. **They** just loved to roll around in the mud.
- Touch the word that's underlined. ✔
Everybody, what word is underlined? **(Signal.)** *They.*
- What was Mrs. Hudson really writing about? **(Signal.)** *The pigs.*
- What did Zelda think she was writing about? **(Signal.)** *Mrs. Hudson's brother and sister.*
3. Listen: Cross out the word **they** and write **my brother and sister** above the crossed-out word. Raise your hand when you're finished.
(Observe children and give feedback.)

4. Touch number 2. ✔
I'll read what it says: We always kept a glass on top of the refrigerator. We kept it full of water.

- Touch the word that's underlined. ✔
Everybody, what word is underlined? (Signal.) *It.*

- What was Mrs. Hudson really writing about? (Signal.) *The glass.*

- What did Zelda think she was writing about? (Signal.) *The refrigerator.*

- Listen: Cross out the word **it** and write **the refrigerator.** Raise your hand when you're finished.
(Observe children and give feedback.)

5. Now the sentences for both pictures tell what Zelda thought she should illustrate. Later you can color the pictures.

6. When you're done, you will have finished your first workbook. In the next lesson, you'll start a brand-new workbook.

There are three reasons for providing children with practice in making ambiguous sentences.

1. They find it to be a lot of fun.
2. It helps children understand the difference between the clear sentence and the ambiguous counterpart. The ambiguous sentence that children write as a "joke" is often the same sentence those children write when they are trying to be clear.
3. The work that children produce gives good evidence that they understand which words are potentially confusing.

In later lessons, children construct ambiguous sentence pairs that do not have prompted parts. For example, in lesson 47, children work with pairs of sentences. They identify the part of the second sentence that names something. They then use the appropriate pronouns to make the second sentence ambiguous. Here are the items.

c.
1. The boys played with dogs. The dogs had short tails.

2. The girls went in boats. The boats were made of wood.

3. The truck went up a hill. The truck had a flat tire.

Here is the last part of the exercise. (Children have crossed out the first part of the second sentence in each item.)

5. (Write on the board:)

He She It They

- To make the sentences confusing, you use one of these words. The words are **he, she, it, they.**
- You have to pick the right word to start the second sentence in each item.
- Touch item 1. ✔
Everybody, what did you cross out in the second sentence? (Signal.) *The dogs.*
- You can use one of the words on the board to tell about the boys or the dogs. Raise your hand when you know which word that is.
- Everybody, which word? (Signal.) *They.*
- Yes, **they.** Write the word **they** above the crossed-out words.
(Observe children and give feedback.)
- I'll read what item 1 should say now: The boys played with dogs. **They** had short tails.
- Now we don't know who had short tails. Maybe it was the dogs. Maybe it was . . . (pause) . . . **the boys.**

6. Item 2. The girls went in boats. The boats were made of wood.
- What did you cross out in the second sentence? (Signal.) *The boats.*
- You can use one of the words on the board to tell about the girls or the boats. Raise your hand when you know which word that is.
- Everybody, which word? (Signal.) *They.*
- Yes, they. Write the word **they** above the crossed-out words. Raise your hand when you're finished.
- I'll read what item 2 should say now: The girls went in boats. **They** were made of wood.
- Now we don't know what was made of wood. Maybe it was the boats. Maybe it was . . . (pause) . . . **the girls.**

7. Item 3: The truck went up a hill. The truck had a flat tire.
- What did you cross out in the second sentence? (Signal.) *The truck.*
- You can use one of the words on the board to tell about the truck or the hill. Raise your hand when you know which word that is.
- Everybody, which word? (Signal.) *It.*
- Yes, it. Write the word **it** above the crossed-out words. Raise your hand when you're finished.
- I'll read what item 3 should say now: The truck went up a hill. **It** had a flat tire.
- Now we don't know what had a flat tire. Maybe it was the truck. Maybe it was . . . (pause) . . . **the hill.**
8. There is a big box at the bottom of the page.
- Later you can draw a picture in that box to show how Zelda might illustrate one of those items.

Teaching Note

Make sure that children give strong verbal responses in steps 5 through 7. Often children are vague about the name that replaces "the dogs" or "the truck." If children give weak responses, go back to the beginning of step 5 and repeat the verbal work.

The focus of many clarity activities in Level B is on finding the ambiguity or the unintended meaning. The unintended meaning may be humorous. Children who do the various clarity activities in Level B learn this "game." It will help them greatly in both their future reading comprehension and in their writing.

Relative Size

Level B presents exercises involving relative size. The reason is that relative size assumes that one can take a particular viewpoint. A skyscraper is large when compared to us. The same building is tiny when compared to Pike's Peak.

Children in Level B learn about size perspective through a story involving Owen (a giant) and Fizz and Liz (people who are about one inch tall). Various relative-size exercises are generated from this story. For some activities, children view the world from the perspective of Owen. For others, they look at it as Fizz and Liz see it.

The work on relative size starts in lesson 12. Here's the first part of an exercise from lesson 19. Children describe things from the viewpoint of Fizz and Liz.

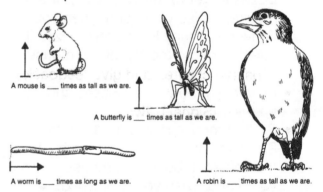

A mouse is ___ times as tall as we are.

A butterfly is ___ times as tall as we are.

A worm is ___ times as long as we are.

A robin is ___ times as tall as we are.

Along the side of the page is a pile of Fizzes and Lizzes.
- Cut out the whole strip. Cut along the dotted lines. Raise your hand when you're finished.
(Observe children and give feedback.)
2. I'll read what it says under each animal.
- Everybody, touch the **mouse.** ✔ It says: A mouse is blank times as tall as we are. It doesn't tell how many times.
- Touch the **butterfly.** ✔ It says: A butterfly is blank times as tall as we are.
- Touch the **robin.** ✔ It says: A robin is blank times as tall as we are.

- Touch the **worm**. ✔
  It says: A worm is blank times as long as we are.
- You're going to use your pile of Fizzes and Lizzes to figure out how they would describe the animals in the picture.
- You'll fill in the blanks with the right numbers.

3. Everybody, touch the **mouse** again. ✔
   Next to the mouse is a mark with an arrow going up from it. Put your pile of Fizzes and Lizzes on that mark and make the pile go in the same direction as the arrow. Put your pile so the **bottom** is right on the mark and the pile goes up. Raise your hand when your pile is in place.
   (Observe children and give feedback.)

4. Now you can start at the bottom of the pile and count the number of Fizzes and Lizzes to get to the very **top** of the mouse. Raise your hand when you know how many Fizzes and Lizzes it takes to get to the top of the mouse.
   (Observe children and give feedback.)
- Everybody, how many Fizzes and Lizzes? (Signal.) *Two.*
- So that mouse is **two** times as tall as Fizz and Liz. Write **two** in the blank in the sentence below the mouse. Raise your hand when you're finished. ✔

5. Everybody, touch the **butterfly**. ✔
   Put your pile so the bottom of the pile is on the line next to the butterfly. Then see how many Fizzes and Lizzes it takes to get to the very **top** of that butterfly's wing. Write the number for the butterfly then write the number for the robin. Then stop. Don't do the worm. Raise your hand when you have numbers for the butterfly and the robin.
   (Observe children and give feedback.)
- Everybody, touch the butterfly.
- Everybody, how many Fizzes and Lizzes is the butterfly? (Signal.) *Three.*
- Here's what your sentence should say: A butterfly is **three** times as tall as we are.

The problems that children encounter in exercises that require cutting and measuring are:

1. They work slowly and inaccurately.
2. They don't position their strips correctly (step 3).

To make the activity move, make sure that children have scissors before the exercise begins.

When children have finished cutting, they should put their scissors aside and hold up their strip to show they're finished. Praise children who finish quickly. If some children are working very slowly, present the rest of the activity to the children who are ready (starting with step 2).

In step 3, observe children carefully. The pile should be right side up. The bottom of the pile should be on the mark. Some children may have trouble identifying the top of the object they are measuring. If a child has trouble, tell the child, "Touch the very top of the mouse, then move your finger straight over to your strip. That's where you stop counting. That's the top of the mouse." If children follow the steps of positioning the strip, identifying the top of the object, and moving to the strip, they quickly catch on to how to measure. Without specific instruction, however, some of them remain quite confused.

Time, Rate and Distance

Children typically have serious knowledge deficits with respect to units of time, rate and distance. Typically, the second grader doesn't understand the difference between "miles" and "miles an hour." They also have trouble with a lot of the concepts associated with these units. For example, children have trouble understanding that if a picture shows two characters racing, the character in front might be going more slowly than the character who is behind. For the children, the faster character is in front. Also, children have great trouble with the inverse relationships, the idea that if somebody is faster, that person will finish a race in less time than a slower racer. This fact is particularly paradoxical to many children because the faster racer goes a greater distance during a period of time. (A greater distance has a larger number. So why does the time have a smaller number?)

Much of the work that children will later do in reading, math, science and other content areas assumes knowledge of the concepts of rate, time and distance.

Level B teaches how these concepts are related. The track starts with what the children already know about faster and slower and presents a series of graded tasks that introduce different "races."

Lesson 42 presents a race between a mouse and a turtle. The racetrack shows the second markers for each racer. Children indicate where the racers are after a specified number of seconds. Here's the introductory exercise.

1. You're going to work some hard problems that tell how fast characters go. For these problems, you have to understand how much time a second is.
 - (Present clock with second hand.) Each line is a second. So each time the hand crosses a line, a second goes by. I'll count the seconds. Watch the hand. 1 . . . 2 . . . 3 . . . 4 . . . 5.

2. Your turn: Start with one and count 5 seconds. Get ready. (Signal.) 1 . . . 2 . . . 3 . . . 4 . . . 5.

Workbook Activity

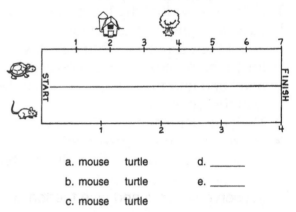

a. mouse	turtle	d. _____
b. mouse	turtle	e. _____
c. mouse	turtle	

1. The picture shows a turtle and a mouse getting ready to race.
 - Touch the turtle. ✔ The numbers above the turtle's lane show where the turtle will be after the turtle and the mouse have raced for 1 second, for 2 seconds, for 3 seconds and so forth.
 - Touch where the turtle will be after 1 second. To do that, you touch the 1 above the turtle's lane.
 - Touch where the turtle will be after 2 seconds. ✔
 - Go to the end of the turtle's lane and touch the last number for the turtle. ✔
 - Everybody, what's the last number for the turtle? (Signal.) 7.
 - That means it will take the turtle 7 seconds to get to the finish line.

2. Now touch the mouse. ✔ The numbers below the mouse's lane show where the mouse will be after 1 second, 2 seconds, 3 seconds and 4 seconds.
 - Touch the number that shows where the mouse will be after 1 second. To do that, you touch the 1 below the mouse's lane. ✔
 - Touch the number that shows where the mouse will be after 2 seconds. ✔
 - Touch the number at the end of the mouse's lane. ✔

- Everybody, what's the number? (Signal.) *4.*
- That means it will take the mouse 4 seconds to get to the finish line. That mouse goes a lot faster than the turtle.
3. Let's pretend that the mouse and the turtle are getting ready to race. I'll count the seconds. When I stop, you'll touch the number for the mouse with one hand and the number for the turtle with the other hand.
- They are getting ready. Go. 1 . . . 2.
- Touch where the mouse is after 2 seconds and where the turtle is after 2 seconds.
  (Observe children and give feedback.)
- Everybody, who is ahead after 2 seconds? (Signal.) *The mouse.*
- One character is at the barn after 2 seconds. Everybody, which character is that? (Signal.) *The turtle.*
- One character is at the tree. Everybody, which character is that? (Signal.) *The mouse.*
4. New race. This time you're going to circle where the characters are. They are at the starting line. They are getting ready. Go. 1 . . . 2 . . . 3 . . . 4.
- Touch where the mouse is after 4 seconds and where the turtle is after 4 seconds. ✔
- Circle the mouse's 4 and the turtle's 4 to show where they are after 4 seconds. Raise your hand when you're finished.
  (Observe children and give feedback.)
- Everybody, where is the mouse after 4 seconds? (Signal.) *At the finish line.*
- The turtle is next to something after 4 seconds. What is the turtle next to? (Signal.) *The tree.*
5. Touch the names under the picture. ✔ You're going to circle the answer to some items.

- Item A: Who ran faster, the mouse or the turtle? Circle the right name. Circle mouse or turtle to tell who ran faster. Raise your hand when you're finished.
  (Observe children and give feedback.)
- Item B: Who ran slower, the mouse or the turtle? Circle the right name. Raise your hand when you're finished. ✔
- Item C: Who reached the finish line **first,** the mouse or the turtle? Circle the right name. Raise your hand when you're finished. ✔
6. For the last items, you'll write numbers. Here's item D. Listen: How many seconds did it take the turtle to get as far as the tree? Listen again: How many seconds did it take the **turtle** to get as far as the tree? Write the number that shows how many seconds it took the turtle to get to the tree. Raise your hand when you're finished. ✔
- Here's item E. How many seconds did it take the **mouse** to get as far as the tree? Write the number that shows how many seconds it took the mouse to get to the tree. Raise your hand when you're finished. ✔
7. Let's see how well you did on those questions:
- Item A: Who ran faster? Everybody, what's the answer? (Signal.) *The mouse.*
- Item B: Who ran slower? (Signal.) *The turtle.*
- Item C: Who reached the finish line first? (Signal.) *The mouse.*
- Item D: How many seconds did it take the turtle to reach the tree? (Signal.) *4.*
- Item E: How many seconds did it take the mouse to reach the tree? (Signal.) *2.*
- The mouse got to the tree in only 2 seconds, but it took the turtle 4 seconds.
8. Raise your hand if you got everything right.

Teaching Note

The children shouldn't have any serious problems with this exercise. The tasks that are presented make it easy for children to track how far each character goes in the same amount of time. This is relatively easy for the children. The questions that are presented after they "act out" different races show that time may be a variable. Items D and E ask how far it took the racers to get to the **same place**—the tree. By working this and similar problems, children learn that the slower runner has the larger number of seconds. The mouse reached the tree in only two seconds. The turtle reached the tree in four seconds.

Children work on exercises similar to the race above in lessons 43 and 44. In lesson 45, a new variation of the racetrack is introduced. This racetrack has lines that mark the feet. The children know that the numbers mark the amount of time it takes each racer to reach the finish line. Children first act out the race as they had on previous exercises. Then they deal with the information presented by the feet markers. Here's the activity from lesson 45.

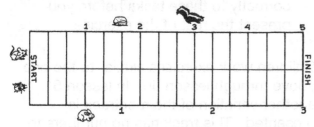

This is another one of those races. Bertha is going to race a mouse. If you look at the numbers for Bertha and the mouse, you'll see who is faster. Remember, the faster racer is the one who goes farther each second.

- Everybody, who is faster? (Signal.) *Bertha.*
- Look at the finish line.
- How many seconds does it take Bertha to reach the finish line? (Signal.) *3.*
- How many seconds does it take the mouse to reach the finish line? (Signal.) *5.*
- Remember, the faster runner gets to the finish line first. Everybody, who reaches the finish line first? (Signal.) *Bertha.*
- Bertha gets there a lot sooner than the mouse.

2. Touch Bertha and the mouse at the starting line. ✔
- They're getting ready to race. I'll count the seconds. Get ready. Go. 1 . . . 2 . . . 3.
- Touch the numbers that show where both the racers are after 3 seconds. ✔
- Where is Bertha after 3 seconds? (Signal.) *At the finish line.*
- Yes, she finished. She's out of here.
- Where is the mouse? (Signal.) *Next to the skunk.*

3. This race track has lines across it. Each line shows 1 foot. Start at the start line and count those feet markers all the way to the finish line. Then you'll know how many feet long that whole track is. Count the feet markers to the finish line. Raise your hand when you know the number of feet for the whole track.
- Everybody, how many feet long is the whole track? (Signal.) *15.*
- Yes, it's 15 feet long.
- Listen: Go back to the start line and count the number of feet to the rabbit. Raise your hand when you know how far it is to the rabbit.
- Everybody, how many feet to the rabbit? (Signal.) *3.*
- Listen: One of the runners gets to the rabbit in 1 second. Raise your hand when you know who is at the rabbit in 1 second. Everybody, who is that? (Signal.) *The mouse.*

- Listen: The mouse reaches the rabbit in 1 second. The rabbit is 3 feet from the start line. So the mouse runs 3 feet in 1 second. That's how fast the mouse runs. 3 feet in 1 second.
4. How **fast** does the mouse run? (Signal.) *3 feet in 1 second.*
(Repeat step 4 until firm.)
5. Bertha runs faster. She runs more than 3 feet in 1 second. Count the number of feet Bertha runs in 1 second. Raise your hand when you know how many feet she runs in 1 second.
- Everybody, how many feet does Bertha run in 1 second? (Signal.) *5 feet.*
- That's how **fast** she runs. 5 feet in 1 second. How **fast** does she run? (Signal.) *5 feet in 1 second.*
6. Listen: The mouse runs 3 feet in 1 second. Bertha runs 5 feet in 1 second. So who runs more feet in 1 second? (Signal.) *Bertha.*
- So Bertha is faster.
7. Get ready to circle names to answer some questions.
- Item A: Which runner went 5 feet in 1 second? Circle the name. Raise your hand when you're finished. ✔
- Item B: Which runner went 3 feet in 1 second? Circle the name. Raise your hand when you're finished. ✔
- Item C: Which runner was ahead after 1 second? Circle the name. Raise your hand when you're finished. ✔
8. For the rest of the questions, you'll write numbers or names.
- Item D: How many seconds did it take the mouse to reach the skunk? Write the number. Raise your hand when you're finished. ✔
- Item E: This is tough. How many feet is it from the start line to the skunk? Count the feet from the start line to the skunk and write the number. Raise your hand when you're finished. ✔
- Item F: Who was the first character to reach the rock? Write the name. Raise your hand when you're finished. ✔

9. Check your work.
- Item A: Which runner went 5 feet in 1 second? (Signal.) *Bertha.*
- Item B: Which runner went 3 feet in 1 second? (Signal.) *The mouse.*
- Item C: Which runner was ahead after 1 second? (Signal.) *Bertha.*
- Item D: How many seconds did it take the mouse to reach the skunk? (Signal.) *3.*
- Item E: How many feet is it from the start line to the skunk? (Signal.) *9.*
- Item F: Who was the first character to reach the rock? (Signal.) *Bertha.*
10. Raise your hand if you got everything right.

Teaching Note

Children are typically confused by questions that refer to how fast, how far or how long. In step 4, children tell how fast the mouse goes. In step 5, they tell about Bertha. In step 6, they answer a question about who was faster. If children are not firm on any part of these sequences, return to the bullet just before step 4 and repeat from that part through step 6. Repeat this part of the exercise several times, if necessary. Make sure that children are responding correctly to these tasks before you present the rest of the exercise.

Children work exercises similar to the one above through lesson 50. In lesson 51, another variation of the racetrack is presented. This track has no numbers to mark the seconds it takes each runner to complete the race. Instead, it has a rule box that tells about the number of feet each runner goes. Children write numbers to show the seconds. They then answer questions about the race. Next is the activity from lesson 51.

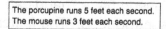
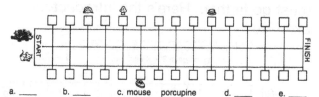

a. ____   b. ____   c. mouse   porcupine   d. ____   e. ____

Here's a track showing a race between the porcupine and the mouse. But somebody forgot to write the numbers telling how long it took each animal to reach things.

2. Touch the sentences in the box above the track. ✔
   Those sentences tell the rules about how fast the racers go.
   • I'll read what it says about **the porcupine.** Follow along. The porcupine runs 5 feet each second.
   • How many feet does the porcupine run each second? **(Signal.)** *5.*
   • You're going to put in the second markers for the porcupine. Remember, they go above the porcupine lane.
   • The porcupine runs 5 feet each second. Start at the start line. Count the 5 feet for the first second and write number 1. Then start at that mark and count 5 more feet and make another number. Make a number every 5 feet to the finish line. Raise your hand when you're finished.
   (Observe children and give feedback.)

3. Everybody, touch number 1. ✔
   Number 1 should be right by the toadstool. Raise your hand if you got it right.
   • Touch number 2. ✔
   That number should be right by Roger's hat. Raise your hand if you got it right.
   • Touch the last number you made. Everybody, where is that mark?
   (Signal.) *At the finish line.*
   • Yes, at the finish line.

4. I'll read the fact about the mouse in the rule box: The mouse runs 3 feet each second.

   • Your turn: Start at the start line. Count 3 feet and write number 1. Make numbers every 3 feet to the finish line. Remember to make your numbers below the mouse's lane. Raise your hand when you're finished.
   (Observe children and give feedback.)

5. Touch number 1 for the mouse. That number should be right below the rock. Raise your hand if you got it right.
   • Touch number 2.
   That number should be right by the shoe. Raise your hand if you got it right.
   • Everybody, how many seconds does it take the mouse to finish the race?
   (Signal.) *5.*

6. Let's see how that race goes. The racers are at the start line. Get ready. Go. 1 . . . 2.
   • Touch where each racer is.
   • Which racer is ahead after 2 seconds? **(Signal.)** *The porcupine.*
   • What's the porcupine next to after 2 seconds? **(Signal.)** *Roger's hat.*
   • What's the mouse next to? **(Signal.)** *The shoe.*

7. Let's start the race again: The racers are at the start line. Get ready. Go. 1 . . . 2. . . . 3.
   • Where is the porcupine? **(Signal.)** *At the finish line.*
   • Raise your hand when you know how many feet the mouse is from the finish line.
   • Everybody, how many feet is the mouse from the finish line? **(Signal.)** *6.*
   • So that mouse still has 6 feet to go and the porcupine is already at the finish line.

8. Get ready to write answers to items.
   • Item A: How many feet did the porcupine run each second?
   • Item B: How many feet did the mouse run each second?
   • Item C: Who finished the race first? Circle the name.

- Item D: How many seconds did it take the porcupine to finish the race?
- Item E: How many seconds did it take the mouse to finish the race?
9. Check your work.
   - Item A: How many feet did the porcupine run each second? (Signal.) *5.*
   - Item B: How many feet did the mouse run each second? (Signal.) *3.*
   - Item C: Who finished the race first? (Signal.) *The porcupine.*
   - Item D: How many seconds did it take the porcupine to finish the race? (Signal.) *3.*
   - Item E: How many seconds did it take the mouse to finish the race? (Signal.) *5.*
10. Raise your hand if you got everything right.

Teaching Notes

In step 2, children are to write the numbers for the porcupine's seconds. Some children make the mistake of counting before they move. Have them start at the start line. Remind them not to count before they start moving. Then have them count five places.

Notice that the tasks are getting more difficult. But if the preceding work has been done carefully, the children should not have serious problems with any tasks. In this race, children count the number of **feet** the mouse has gone when the porcupine is at the finish line (step 7).

Starting in lesson 54, a "handicap" racetrack is introduced. The faster runner must go farther. Here's the introductory exercise.

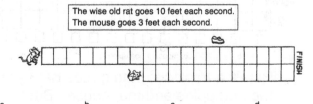

The wise old rat goes 10 feet each second.
The mouse goes 3 feet each second.

a. _____ b. _____ c. _____ d. _____

This is a new kind of race. The wise old rat is going to race with the mouse. But the mouse has a big head start.
- Look at where the mouse is starting. It looks like that mouse might just win that race. We'll find out.
- Touch the box that gives rules about the racers.
- I'll read the rule about the wise old rat. Follow along: The wise old rat goes 10 feet each second. That's pretty far.
- I'll read the rule about the mouse. Follow along: The mouse goes 3 feet each second.
- How many feet does the mouse go each second? (Signal.) *3.*
- How many feet does the wise old rat go each second? (Signal.) *10.*
2. The wise old rat goes 10 feet each second. Put in the marks for the wise old rat's seconds. Then write the numbers. Raise your hand when you're finished.
   (Observe children and give feedback.)
   - Everybody, how many second marks do you have for the wise old rat? (Signal.) *2.*
3. The mouse goes 3 feet each second. Start at the start line for the mouse and put in the marks for the mouse's seconds. Then write the numbers. Raise your hand when you're finished.
   (Observe children and give feedback.)
   - Everybody, how many second marks do you have for the mouse? (Signal.) *4*

4. Let's see how that race goes. The racers are each at their start line.
- Touch both racers. ✔
  Get ready. Go. 1.
- Touch the 1-second mark for each racer. ✔
- Who is ahead after 1 second? (Signal.) *The mouse.*
- How many feet behind is the wise old rat? (Signal.) *1.*
- That wise old rat really caught up a lot.
- Go back to the start lines.
- Touch both racers. ✔
- Get ready. Go. 1 . . . 2.
- Touch the 2-second mark for each racer. ✔
- Where is the wise old rat after 2 seconds? (Signal.) *At the finish line.*
- Where is the mouse after 2 seconds? (Signal.) *Next to the shoe.*
- That head start doesn't do that mouse a lot of good. She's only at the shoe when the wise old rat finishes the race.
5. Get ready to write answers to some items.
- Item A: How many seconds did it take the wise old rat to finish the race? Write the number.
- Item B: The wise old rat finished the race in 2 seconds. When the wise old rat finished the race, how many feet was the mouse from the finish line? Find the 2-second mark for the mouse and figure out how many feet she was from the finish line. Raise your hand when you've written your answer.
- Item C: How many feet did the wise old rat go each second?
- Item D: How many feet did the mouse go each second?
6. Check your work.
- Item A: How many seconds did it take the wise old rat to finish the race? (Signal.) *2.*
- Item B: When the wise old rat finished the race, how many feet was the mouse from the finish line? (Signal.) *6.*
- Item C: How many feet did the wise old rat go each second? (Signal.) *10.*

- Item D: How many feet did the mouse go each second? (Signal.) *3.*

Teaching Note

The amount of structure provided is greatly reduced and the questions are becoming increasingly difficult, but the children should have no trouble. This type of race addresses the problem children have in understanding that the person who is behind could be going faster.

Starting in lesson 66, children discriminate between verbal statements of "speed," statements of "time," and statements of "distance." They also construct rules for racers' rates. By lesson 66, children have worked with races that show inches, feet and miles. The race in lesson 66 is in miles. Here's the exercise.

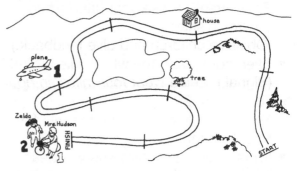

1. Zelda went _____.
2. Mrs. Hudson went _____.
3. _____ 4. at the _____ 5. _____ 6. _____

This is really difficult. Here's a race that is already finished. Both the racers are standing around at the finish line. You're going to figure out the facts for this race and answer questions.
2. This race is in miles.
- Touch Zelda at the finish line. The number in red tells how many hours it took her to finish the race. Everybody, how many hours? (Signal.) *Two.*

- If you look at the mile markers, you'll see where Zelda was at the end of one hour. Find the number 1 for Zelda. It's in red. Where was Zelda at the end of one hour? (Signal.) *At the plane.*
- Where was Zelda at the end of two hours? (Signal.) *At the finish line.*

3. Touch Mrs. Hudson.
   She rode her bike. The number in blue tells how many hours it took her to reach the finish line. Everybody, how many hours? (Signal.) *One.*

4. (Write on the board:)

miles an hour

- Touch the space for item 1.
  You're going to complete the rule for Zelda. You'll tell how fast Zelda went. That's how many miles an hour she went.
- Count the miles to Zelda's one-hour marker, and you'll know how fast she went. Write how many miles an hour Zelda went. Raise your hand when you're finished.
  (Observe children and give feedback.)
- Everybody, read the whole rule for Zelda. (Signal.) *Zelda went four miles an hour.*

5. Touch item 2.
   You're going to complete the rule for Mrs. Hudson.
- Write how many miles she went each hour. Count the miles to her one-hour marker, and you'll know how fast she went. Raise your hand when you're finished.
  (Observe children and give feedback.)
- Everybody, read the whole rule for Mrs. Hudson. (Signal.) *Mrs. Hudson went eight miles an hour.*

6. Item 3: Who won the race? Write the name. Raise your hand when you're finished.
   (Observe children and give feedback.)
- Everybody, who won the race? (Signal.) *Mrs. Hudson.*

7. Item 4: Tell where Zelda was when Mrs. Hudson reached the finish line. Write the name of the place. Raise your hand when you're finished.
   (Observe children and give feedback.)
- Everybody, where was Zelda when Mrs. Hudson finished the race? (Signal.) *At the plane.*

8. Item 5: Tell how many hours it took Zelda to finish the race. Write the answer. Raise your hand when you're finished.
   (Observe children and give feedback.)
- Everybody, how many hours did it take Zelda to finish the race? (Signal.) *Two.*

9. Item 6: Tell how many hours it took Mrs. Hudson to finish the race. Write the answer. Raise your hand when you're finished.
   (Observe children and give feedback.)
- Everybody, how many hours did it take Mrs. Hudson to finish the race? (Signal.) *1.*

Cooperative Activities

COMPOSITION AND PLAYS

For some activities in Level B, children work cooperatively in groups to compose episodes involving familiar story characters or to stage plays that show part of a familiar story.

The activities specified in the program are fun. They serve as a model for additional plays or for cooperatively developed compositions you might have the children do after they have completed Level B.

For cooperative story writing, children work in groups. The children are provided with a series of questions that they are to answer in constructing their story. They plan the story during part of one lesson. During the following lesson(s), they present their story.

In lessons 27 and 28, children work on composing their first story. Next is an activity from both lessons.

Lesson 27

Note: Divide the class into teams of 3–4 children.

You're going to work in teams and make up a story that tells what happened when Fizz and Liz went to visit Owen. There are pictures of things with question marks after them.
(Write on the board:)

?

- Here's a question mark.
2. Everybody, touch the top picture. ✔ It shows Fizz and Liz. Then there's a question mark. That means you have to tell something about **who** went to Owen's island. Did just Fizz and Liz go or did **some** of the other little people go with them? Or did **all** of the little people go? That's the first thing you'll tell in your story.

- Touch the next picture. ✔
That's a racing boat. The question mark asks about the racing boat: Did they go to Owen's island in their racing boat? Or did they go in the green bottle? Or did they make some other kind of boat? Or did they go in the bottle and pull some of the racing boats behind? You have to tell **how** they decided to go to Owen's island.
- Touch the picture of the berries. ✔ The berries might be something they would eat. But you'll have to tell what they brought with them to eat. Remember, they'll be out on the waves for **six** days.
- Is that right? (Signal.) *No.*
- How long will they be on the ocean? (Signal.) *Three days.*
- They'll need supplies for their journey. We don't want them to die of thirst out there in the ocean. Remember, they can't drink ocean water—it's too salty and would make them sick. So you have to tell **what** they took with them.
- Touch the next picture. ✔
- It shows a note. The question mark asks **how** did they let Owen know they were coming? Or maybe they just dropped in on Owen, without letting him know they were coming. If they did that, they might just get stepped on by one of those giants. So your story will have to tell something about **how** they let Owen know they were coming to his island.
- Touch the next picture. ✔
- That picture shows the direction they would go from their island to Owen's island. The question mark asks **what happened** on their trip. You should tell about what they did during the three days they were on the water. You could even mention the direction they were going to.
- Everybody, what direction were they going to? (Signal.) *East.*

- Touch the last picture. ✔
  That picture shows Owen holding a couple of little people. The question mark means **what happened** when they finally got to Owen's island. You should probably tell at least some of the things they did.
3. Everybody, we're going to work in teams. Here's how you'll work in teams: For each picture, team members will give suggestions to their team.
- First, you'll decide **who** went to Owen's island. But, don't argue. If you don't agree, go to the next picture and see if you can work out something for that picture. Later in the story, you may have some ideas that will help you to figure out what you want for the earlier picture.
- After you figure out **what** your story will tell for each picture, you'll have a good story.
4. All teams, start with picture 1. Figure out who went to Owen's island.
- **(Observe each team. Ask:)** Have you figured out **who** went on the trip?
- Then go on to the next picture and figure out **how** they went on their trip.
  (Praise teams who are discussing possibilities and working cooperatively.)
- Raise your hand if your team figured out answers to all the questions.
- **(Repeat step 4 for each picture.)**
5. In the next lesson, you'll figure out how your team is going to tell their story to the whole class. Maybe one team member will tell the first part, another team member will tell the next part, and so on. Maybe one person will tell the whole story. Next time, you'll figure out how you're going to do it. Then we'll have each team tell their story about the trip to Owen's island.
6. You can draw things on this page to help you remember your story.

Note: Divide the class into teams of 3–4 children.

1. Everybody, find part D in lesson **27**. ✔ Remember, these pictures ask questions about important parts of your story.
- Today, we're going to hear stories from the different groups. Before we do that, the groups have to figure out how they'll tell their story.
2. Get together with the same group as last time and figure out how you'll do it. Then you should practice your story in your group before you present it to the class. You should make sure your story answers all the questions.
- If different children are telling different parts, practice telling the story. The other members of the group should listen carefully and make sure that each storyteller is telling it the right way.
- Talk quietly so that the other groups can't hear your story.
  (Observe groups and give feedback. Praise groups who practice and comment on the storyteller's rendition.)
3. Raise your hand when your group is ready. The first group ready gets to tell their story first.
4. **(Call on a group, say:)** Everybody, listen to the story from group ___.
  (Praise stories that tell about the details suggested by the pictures.)

Note: If not all the groups are able to present, tell the class that the storytelling will be continued in the next lesson.

Teaching Notes

Create groups that have some diversity in ability. Each group should have a higher–performing student, several average performers and possibly a lower performer. Don't construct groups that have only lower performers.

On the second day, the groups work together before presenting to the class. Praise groups that rehearse their presentation. Ask the groups questions if they seem lost. "Have you decided how they are going to get to Owen's island? Who is going to tell that part of the story? Tell that part to me very quietly . . . "

When children present, tell the listeners in the class to point to the various questions on the checklist to see if the presentation answers all the questions.

EXPANDED ACTIVITIES

By the time you complete the program, you'll have a good idea about how to handle these projects in a way that builds naturally on what the children already know. You'll know which things children may need more work on and which things would be fun (such as developing a large, illustrated book).

Projects that require the use and integration of reading, writing, thinking and listening will be relatively easy for the children because they will have the component reasoning skills and will be facile in applying them.

The program offers some suggestions about early activities. For instance, lesson 14 provides an optional activity for children to create a picture book. Children complete a picture to show their favorite part of the story.

1. Everybody, find part D.
   In that space, you can draw a picture of your favorite part of the story. Maybe your favorite part is when the mouse covers the toad. Maybe your favorite part is when they're both snoring. Maybe your favorite part is when they argue.
2. Draw your favorite part. Maybe we'll make a picture book for the story.

Children can work cooperatively to create a picture book to show the entire story. Good pictures are arranged in the same order as the major events of the story. Additional pictures are created if important parts of the story are missing. A pair of children can then put on a "show" to the class, in which one child turns the pages and shows the pictures to the class while another child recounts the story.

Following lesson 31, children have been prepared for optional sentence-writing activities. The simplest format is the one used in the program. Children refer to the **Story words** page in their workbook.

Story words

Present a model sentence such as:

_____ wanted to buy _____.

or

_____ sat on top of _____.

Children use the Story words to generate sentences of the form shown.

At the end of lesson 70 is an activity in which children vote for different things they would like to do next. The choices presented are: story writing, plays, books, maps.

Extra Activities

A   Story Writing

1. ___ Dessera
2. ___ Dot and Dud
3. ___ Dooly
4. ___ Sherlock
5. ___ Zelda and Mrs. Hudson
6. ___ Owen, Fizz and Liz
7. ___ _____

B   Plays

1. ___ Dot and Dud with the Greyhounds
2. ___ Mrs. Hudson and Zelda
3. ___ Dooly and Caw-Caw
4. ___ Bleep and Molly
5. ___ Owen Visiting Fizz and Liz
6. ___ _____

C   Books

1. ___ A book by Mrs. Hudson and Zelda
2. ___ Letters sent to Owen and Fizz and Liz
3. ___ A book of silly Bleep-talk
4. ___ _____

D   Maps

1. ___ Our school
2. ___ Our neighborhood
3. ___ Our classroom
4. ___ _____

1. Find the section in your workbook called **Extra Activities.** It's the page right after your test. We don't have any more lessons in this program. But we will work on some activities. You can vote on the things you want to do.
2. Touch part A: Story Writing. ✔
   You'll get to choose who you would like to write a story about.
   • I'll read the choices: Dessera, Dot and Dud, Dooly, Sherlock, Zelda and Mrs. Hudson, Owen and Fizz and Liz, and a blank line.

   • Listen: You can choose from one of the items written. Or you can write the name of another character on line 7. Maybe you want Bleep, Zena and Zola, or some other character.
   • Put a check mark after the name you want to write about. Or write the name on the last line. Remember, you can choose only one item to write about. Raise your hand when you're finished.
   (Observe children and give feedback.)
3. Part B. These are choices for plays that we can put on: Dot and Dud with the Greyhounds; Mrs. Hudson and Zelda; Dooly and Caw-Caw; Bleep and Molly; Owen Visiting Fizz and Liz; and a blank line.
   • Make a check after one of the names or write the name of your favorite choice for a play on the bottom line. Remember, you can make only one choice for a play. Raise your hand when you're finished.
   (Observe children and give feedback.)
4. Part C: Books.
   These are your choices for books that we can write and illustrate: a book by Mrs. Hudson and Zelda; letters sent to Owen and Fizz and Liz; a book of silly Bleep-talk; and a blank line.
   • Make your choice for a book that we could make. Raise your hand when you're finished.
   (Observe children and give feedback.)
5. Part D: Maps that we could make. These are your choices: our school; our neighborhood; our classroom; and a blank line.
   • Make your choice for the map you'd prefer. Raise your hand when you're finished.
   (Observe children and give feedback.)

6. (Write on the board:)

Part A Stories		Part B Plays		Part C Books		Part D Maps	
1		1		1		1	
2		2		2		2	
3		3		3		3	
4		4		4		4	
5		5					
6		6					
7							

- I'll say the number of each item. You raise your hand when I say the item number you chose.
- Part A. (Say each number. Count votes and write the number of children after each item number. Repeat for parts B, C and D.)

7. The item with the biggest number in each part is the thing we'll do first. (Announce the first story, first play, first book and first map.)

8. We'll have different groups working on different things at the same time. We'll start with the story, the book and the play. Then we'll have show time when each group can put on their play, read their story, or show us their book.

- You'll get to choose the **first thing** you'll work on.
- Listen: Circle the letter A, B or C on your page to show whether you first want to work on a story, a play or a book. Raise your hand when you've circled the letter for your first choice.

9. (Post 3 sign-up sheets, each with a letter.)

A Story	B Play	C Book
_____	_____	_____
_____	_____	_____
_____	_____	_____

- Raise your hand if you circled A.
- Everybody who chose A will write their name on sign-up sheet A. That group will work together on the story. Everybody who circled A, sign up now. (Direct children to sign-up sheet A.)

- Raise your hand if you circled B.
- Everybody who chose B will write their name on sign-up sheet B and will work together on the play. Everybody who circled B, sign up now. (Direct children to sign-up sheet B.)
- Raise your hand if you circled C.
- Everybody who chose C will write their name on sign-up sheet C and will work together on writing and illustrating the book. Everybody who circled C, sign up now. (Direct children to sign-up sheet C.)

10. (After names are written, assign groups to sit together and discuss their project.)

Teaching Notes

For the first round of expanded activities, children choose between writing a story, staging a play, or preparing a book. Making a map is not presented as a choice for the initial work; however, after children have completed their first project, they should vote for their second activity. The map should be included for this round. Often children can incorporate maps with the activity they first selected. As projects develop, different groups will finish at different times. Following the completion of a project, assign the group members (or the group) to a new project.

Tests

In-program Tests

The in-program tests that appear as every tenth lesson of the program provide a basis for periodically judging the progress of individual children and for awarding grades.

During a test, children should be seated so they cannot copy.

Directions for presenting the test appear as part of each test lesson.

When observing children's performance, make sure that they are following directions, but do not tell them answers to any item or give them hints.

Collect student workbooks and mark the tests. If children do poorly on a test, check their work on preceding lessons to determine whether they had problems with the tested concepts when they were presented earlier in the program. Also note discrepancies. If a child does poorly on a test but did very well on all preceding exercises, the child may have been copying.

Mark each item a child misses on the test. Use the Answer Key as the guide. Any deviations are mistakes.

Count the number of mistakes and enter the number at the top of each child's test.

If the child missed three items, the score is −3.

Before returning the test forms, use your copy of the Reproducible Group Summary Sheet that appears on page 100 and enter the number of errors each child made.

Test Remedies

Test remedies are appropriate for children who miss test items. It is possible to use formulas for administering test remedies (if 30% of the children miss an item, present the remedy); however, the goal of the remedies would be to fix up each child's misunderstanding. Children who make more than one mistake on any part of the test should receive a remedy for that part. One procedure for doing this is to:

1. Repeat an exercise in the program (from one of the preceding 9 lessons) that deals with the difficult skill.
2. Then present the test again or the part of the test on which children had trouble.

Below is a list of exercises that should be repeated for the various parts of the tests. Although the workbook is copyrighted and may not normally be reproduced, you may reproduce the parts of the workbook needed for test remedies. After firming children on the remedies, repeat the test or the part of the test the children failed.

Test	Test Part Failed	Lesson	To remedy, present: Book Exercise	Workbook Part
1	A	9	3	B
	B	3	2	B
	C	3	3	C
2	A	14	2	A
	B	19	2	B
3	A	27	1	A
	B	28	2	B
4	A	38	1	A
	B	34	4	C
	C	33	2	B
5	A	47	1	A
	B	48	1	A
6	A	57	4	C
	B	57	1	A
	C	55	4	D
7	A	69	1	A
	B	65	2	B
	C	64	4	C

Objectives

The objectives on pages 90 to 95 show the development of skills and applications taught in *Reasoning and Writing, Level B.*

The skills and applications are grouped by tracks. The headings indicate the major tracks and the divisions within each track. Each track shows the development of a major topic, such as Story Grammar or Deductions. Typically, a track will have activities that are presented over many different lessons of the program.

The major tracks are:
CLASSIFICATION AND CLUES
SENTENCE CONSTRUCTION
DIRECTIONS (North, South, East, West)
DIALECT
DEDUCTIONS
PERSPECTIVE
SPATIAL ORIENTATION
TEMPORAL SEQUENCING
CLARITY
TIME, RATE AND DISTANCE
REPORTING AND INFERENCE
CORRELATED EVENTS
STORY GRAMMAR

There are divisions within some tracks. Each division is marked by a subheading.

The subheadings for Dialect are
CORRECTING
CREATING AND DISCRIMINATING

The subheadings for Perspective are
RELATIVE SIZE
RELATIVE DIRECTION

The subheadings for Spatial Orientation are
ROUTES
CONNECTED COMPONENTS

The subheadings for Clarity are
CORRECTING AMBIGUITY
CREATING AMBIGUITY
DISCRIMINATING

The subheadings for Story Grammar are
MODEL STORIES
APPLICATION
EXTRAPOLATION

Although the objectives show the various categories and the lessons in which each specific objective is taught, the objectives do not show the interrelationships among the various skills. Specific skills are involved in more than one track. Discrete activities address the teaching of spatial orientation (directions—north, south, east, west), relative direction, relative size, and clarity. However, many activities in the program are difficult to "categorize" because they involve an integration of various skills that are taught.

The story activities present complex perspectives, some of which are not stated objectives. The Goober stories, for instance, present a counterpoint of opposites. Goober is a sensual paradox. (His farm sends out awful smells but also sounds of beautiful music.) The story presents a counterpoint of relative direction. (If the wind blows from the east, the awful odor drifts to the west of his farm.) The Goober stories also present a counterpoint of intent and dialect. People hold their nose in the presence of Goober's farm. What they say is therefore different from what they intend. "You bake dice busic" is not what the speaker is trying to say.

Other stories develop perspectives of relative size (Owen and the Little People), relative distance and direction (Dooly the Duck), clarity of expression (Zelda the Artist), and conclusions about unobserved events (Sherlock and Bertha). All these stories also present perspectives based on motives of different characters.

In summary, the objectives show the various skills and applications that are taught; however, skills and applications developed in one track invariably spill over into other tracks as children use and apply what they have learned.

REVIEW

	Objectives	Lessons
All, Some, None	Answer questions involving **all, some** and **none.**	1
	Fix up pictures to show a true **some** statement.	1, 5
	Fix up pictures to show a true **all** statement.	2, 3
	Cross out objects to make an **all** statement true.	4
	Cross out picture elements to show a true **none** statement.	6
	Write **some** and **none** to complete sentences.	6
	Fix up pictures to show a true **some** statement.	7
If–Then	Apply an if–then rule.	1, 2
	Construct and apply 2 related if–then rules.	8, 9
Left/Right	Follow directions involving **left** and **right.**	1, 2, 5
	Identify letters or objects that are 1st, 2nd or 3rd to the **left** or **right.**	3, 9
True/False	Circle the words **true** or **false** for statements.	1, 5, 7
Seasons	Identify seasons from descriptions.	11–13

CLASSIFICATION and CLUES

Objectives	Lessons
Determine which clue eliminates specific members of a class.	2
Use clues to eliminate specific members of a class.	3, 4
Write appropriate object names under class headings.	5, 7
Develop 2 clues that identify a "mystery" object.	6
Use clues to identify members of a class.	22, 23
Arrange objects in larger and smaller classes.	24, 27
Answer questions about mentally–constructed classes.	32–34
Indicate the number of objects in larger and smaller classes.	35
Write 3 sentences to identify the mystery character.	60–63
Write 4 sentences to identify the mystery character.	64, 65, 68

Objectives   Lessons

SENTENCE CONSTRUCTION

Objectives	Lessons
Construct sentences for different illustrations.	3, 7, 11, 12, 44–47
Construct 3 sentences about story characters.	13, 15, 17
Compose 3 simple stories, each based on the same action topic	21, 26, 31
Optional: Write a group of sentences that are thematically related.	34, 37, 43, 46
Combine subjects and predicates to construct sentences about familiar characters.	48, 49

DIRECTIONS (North, South, East, West)

Objectives	Lessons
Follow directions involving **north** and **south**.	5–7
Follow directions involving **north, south, east, west**.	8, 9, 11, 14, 16, 22, 23
Fix up a map to show north (**N**), south (**S**), east (**E**), west (**W**)	12, 13
Draw arrows to indicate **north, south, east, west**.	14
Use directions about **north, south, east, west** to solve a puzzle.	15, 16
Apply a directional rule to solve a maze.	18, 19
Identify the direction an arrow moves **from** and **to**.	23
Draw arrows to show movement **to** and **from** (**to** the east and **from** the west).	25, 27
Compose directions to show solutions to a map puzzle.	29, 32
Complete directions for going to different locations on a map.	54, 55
Apply a rule about moving south and north to a map of North America.	62

DIALECT

	Objectives	Lessons
Correcting	Edit words to **correct** a character's dialect.	6, 7, 14, 15, 24, 48
Creating and Discriminating	Write what a character says in a picture.	6
	Edit words to **show** a character's dialect.	8, 12, 13, 49, 57

Objectives	Lessons
Make a picture consistent with details of a story by writing sentences that show dialect.	59
Connect different assertions with the appropriate speaker.	68
Write what a character is thinking in a picture.	69

DEDUCTIONS

Say a deduction based on 3 pictures.	8, 9
Say different deductions based on pictures.	11–15, 17, 22, 24, 38
Construct deductions to answer questions.	25, 28, 29, 44
Identify the order of parts in a formally correct deduction.	39
Complete a deduction used in the story.	52, 53
Construct deductions that are formally incorrect.	55
Identify deductions that are formally correct (good) or incorrect.	55

PERSPECTIVE

Relative Size	Edit a letter to show a character's reference to the relative sizes of objects.	12
	Identify speakers from references to the relative size of objects.	16
	Answer questions about relative size	18
	Complete descriptions of relative size.	19
	Write a letter that contains descriptions of relative size.	23
Relative Direction	Complete descriptions involving relative direction.	33–35
	Identify where characters are on a map based on assertions about the direction of a common object.	36, 38, 41, 43
	Identify the characters on a map by their assertions about relative direction.	46, 47
	Complete statements of relative direction based on a map.	56, 61, 62

Objectives	Lessons
Use rules about relative direction to indicate why specific places on a map are not the correct places.	63
Write descriptions of "safe spots" based on rules about relative direction.	64

SPATIAL ORIENTATION

	Objectives	Lessons
Routes	Identify objects that are facing the wrong direction.	16, 17, 34
	Position objects so that they are facing the right direction.	18
	Draw routes that reflect story events.	29, 32
	Circle **true** or **false** for statements that tell whether objects are oriented properly.	35, 41
	Draw routes based on instructions that tell about distance and direction.	36, 37
	Relate the details of a story to a map.	63
	Connect specific story events to a map.	64
Connected Components	Draw arrows to show continuous movement.	19, 22, 25, 33, 69
	Draw arrows to show the movements of connected components.	36
	Draw arrows to show the movement of connected components of a bicycle power train.	37, 38
	Draw arrows to show movement of connected gears.	58, 59, 61
	Draw arrows to show which direction gears and a shaft will move to make a bucket move either up or down.	65, 67

TEMPORAL SEQUENCING

Objectives	Lessons
Complete sentences of the form: Blank happened **after** blank.	27, 28, 34, 63
Identify a specific picture sequence by applying clues about the order of actions shown.	37, 39
Write sentences that use the word **after** and tell what an illustrated character did.	51–53, 63

Objectives	Lessons
Write 2 clues for a mystery sequence.	56
Work cooperatively to write 2 clues for the mystery sequence.	57

CLARITY

	Objectives	Lessons
Correcting Ambiguity	Edit sentences to eliminate pronoun ambiguity.	34, 35
	Rewrite a passage so that it unambiguously reports on what a picture sequence shows.	61
	Edit sentences in a passage to eliminate ambiguity.	62
Creating Ambiguity	Rewrite unambiguous sentence pairs so the second sentence is ambiguous.	47, 51, 54, 65
Discriminating	Use cutouts to change specific details of a picture.	36
	Edit ambiguous sentences to show how a character interpreted them.	37–39, 41–43, 45
	Identify the illustrator of ambiguous sentences.	55

TIME, RATE AND DISTANCE

Objectives	Lessons
Relate the "speed" of a character to the "time" it takes the character to reach a point.	42, 43
Answer questions about the amount of time and the speed of characters in a race.	44
Use information about feet per second and answer questions about the amount of time and speed of characters.	45, 46, 48, 49
Apply rules about characters' rates to a map that shows a race.	51, 52, 64
Apply rules about characters' rates in inches per second to a map.	53
Apply rules about characters' rates to a map that shows one character with a head start.	54, 55, 59, 62
Figure out how far racers will be on a course after 1 hour.	63
Discriminate between statements about how far a character goes and how fast the character goes.	66, 67, 69
Use information about times to formulate rules about characters' rates.	66, 69

Objectives Lessons

REPORTING AND INFERENCE

Indicate whether statements about a picture **report** or **do not report.**	56, 57
Write sentences that report.	57–59
Write sentences that infer something that must have happened between illustrations.	66–69

CORRELATED EVENTS

Use information about correlated events to rank different locations.	66
Complete sentences that refer to correlated events.	67

STORY GRAMMAR

Model Stories	Answer comprehension questions about a story.	1–6, 11, 12, 15–17, 19, 21–26, 28, 29, 31–36, 38, 39, 41, 42, 48, 49, 51–53, 55–59, 61–69
	Listen to a familiar story.	7–10, 13, 14, 18, 20, 27, 30, 37, 40,43–47, 50, 54, 60
Application	Make a picture consistent with the details of a story.	1–5, 8, 9, 11, 17, 41, 42, 44, 53, 56, 65, 69
	Draw a picture based on a familiar story.	14
Extrapolation	Predict the outcome of a story.	23, 55
	Cooperatively compose an episode involving familiar story grammar.	27, 58
	Present a cooperatively–developed episode based on familiar story grammar.	28, 59
	Put on a play to show part of a familiar story.	47, 54
	Plan post-program extension activities.	70

Skills Profile—Page 1

The charts on pages 96 to 99 may be reproduced to make a skills profile for each student. The charts summarize the skills presented in *Reasoning and Writing Level B* and provide space for indicating the date on which the student completes the lessons in which the skills are taught.

Student's name _____

Grade or year in school _____

Teacher's name _____

Starting lesson _____ Date _____

Last lesson completed _____ Date _____

Number of days absent _____

Skills	Taught in these Lessons	Date Lessons Completed	Skills	Taught in these Lessons	Date Lessons Completed
REVIEW			**Seasons**		
All, Some, None			Identifies seasons from descriptions	11-13	
Answers questions involving **all**, **some** and **none**	1		**CLASSIFICATION and CLUES**		
Fixes up pictures to show a true **some** statement	1-5		Determines which clue eliminates specific members of a class	2	
Fixes up pictures to show a true **all** statement	2-3		Uses clues to eliminate specific members of a class	3-4	
Crosses out objects to make an **all** statement true	4		Writes appropriate object names under class headings	5-7	
Crosses out picture elements to show a true **none** statement	6		Develops 2 clues that identify a "mystery" object	6	
Writes **some** and **none** to complete sentences	6		Uses clues to identify members of a class	22-23	
Fixes up pictures to show a true **some** statement	7		Arranges objects in larger and smaller classes	24-27	
If–Then			Answers questions about mentally-constructed classes	32-34	
Applies an if-then rule	1-2		Indicates the number of objects in larger and smaller classes	35	
Constructs and applies 2 related if-then rules	8-9		Writes 3 sentences to identify the mystery character	60-63	
Left/Right			Writes 4 sentences to identify the mystery character	64-68	
Follows directions involving **left** and **right**	1-5		**SENTENCE CONSTRUCTION**		
Identifies letters that are 1st, 2nd or 3rd to the **left** or **right**	3-9		Constructs sentences for different illustrations	3-47	
True/False					
Circles the words **true** or **false** for statements	1-7				

Copyright © by SRA/McGraw-Hill. Permission is granted to reproduce this page for classroom use.

Skills	Taught in these Lessons	Date Lessons Completed	Skills	Taught in these Lessons	Date Lessons Completed
Constructs 3 sentences about story characters	13-17		**Creating and Discriminating** Writes what a character says in a picture	6	
Composes 3 simple stories, each based on the same action topic	21-31		Edits words to **show** a character's dialect	8-57	
Optional: Writes a group of sentences that are thematically related	34-46		Makes a picture consistent with details of a story by writing sentences that show dialect	59	
Combines subjects and predicates to construct sentences about familiar characters	48-49		Connects different assertions with the appropriate speaker	68	
DIRECTIONS—North, South, East, West Follows directions involving **north** and **south**	5-7		Writes what a character is thinking in a picture	69	
Follows directions involving **north, south, east, west**	8-23		**DEDUCTIONS** Says a deduction based on 3 pictures	8-9	
Fixes up a map to show north (**N**), south (**S**), east (**E**), west (**W**)	12-13		Says different deductions based on pictures	11-38	
Draws arrows to indicate n**orth, south, east, west**	14		Constructs deductions to answer questions	25-44	
Uses directions about **north, south, east, west** to solve a puzzle	15-16		Identifies the order of parts in a formally correct deduction	39	
Applies a directional rule to solve a maze	18-19		Completes a deduction used in the story	52-53	
Identifies the direction an arrow moves **from** and **to**	23		Constructs deductions that are formally incorrect	55	
Draws arrows to show movement **to** and **from** (**to** the east and **from** the west)	25-27		Identifies deductions that are formally correct (good) or incorrect	55	
Composes directions to show solutions to a map puzzle	29-32		**PERSPECTIVE** **Relative Size** Edits a letter to show a character's reference to the relative size of objects	12	
Completes directions for going to different locations on a map	54-55		Identifies speakers from references to the relative size of objects	16	
Applies a rule about moving south and north to a map of North America	62		Answers questions about relative size	18	
DIALECT **Correcting** Edits words to **correct** a character's dialect	6-48		Completes descriptions of relative size	19	

Copyright © by SRA/McGraw-Hill. Permission is granted to reproduce this page for classroom use.

Skills	Taught in these Lessons	Date Lessons Completed	Skills	Taught in these Lessons	Date Lessons Complete
Writes a letter that contains descriptions of relative size	23		Draws arrows to show the movements of connected components	36	
Relative Direction Completes descriptions involving relative direction	33-35		Draws arrows to show the movement of connected components of a bicycle power train	37-38	
Identifies where characters are on a map based on assertions about the direction of a common object	36-43		Draws arrows to show movement of connected gears	58-61	
Identifies the characters on a map by their assertions about relative direction	46-47		Draws arrows to show which direction gears and a shaft will move to make a bucket move either up or down	65-67	
Completes statements of relative direction based on a map	56-62		**TEMPORAL SEQUENCING** Completes sentences of the form: Blank happened **after** blank	27-63	
Uses rules about relative direction to indicate why specific places on a map are not the correct places	63		Identifies a specific picture sequence by applying clues about the order of actions shown	37-39	
Writes descriptions of "safe spots" based on rules about relative direction	64		Writes sentences that use the word **after** and tell what an illustrated character did	51-63	
SPATIAL ORIENTATION **Routes** Identifies objects that are facing the wrong direction	16-34		Writes 2 clues for a mystery sequence	56	
Positions objects so that they are facing the right direction	18		Works cooperatively to write 2 clues for the mystery sequence	57	
Draws routes that reflect story events	29-32		**CLARITY** **Correcting Ambiguity** Edits sentences to eliminate pronoun ambiguity	34-35	
Circles **true** or **false** for statements that tell whether objects are oriented properly	35-41		Rewrites a passage so that it unambiguously reports on what a picture sequence shows	61	
Draws routes based on instructions that tell about distance and direction	36-37		Edits sentences in a passage to eliminate ambiguity	62	
Relates the details of a story to a map	63		**Creating Ambiguity** Rewrites unambiguous sentence pairs so the second sentence is ambiguous	47-65	
Connects specific story events to a map	64				
Connected Components Draws arrows to show continuous movement	19-69				

Copyright © by SRA/McGraw-Hill. Permission is granted to reproduce this page for classroom use.

Skills	Taught in these Lessons	Date Lessons Completed	Skills	Taught in these Lessons	Date Lessons Completed
Discriminating			**REPORTING AND INFERENCE**		
Uses cutouts to change specific details of a picture	36		Indicates whether statements about a picture **report** or **do not report**	56-57	
Edits ambiguous sentences to show how a character interpreted them	37-45		Writes sentences that report	57-59	
Identifies the illustrator of ambiguous sentences	55		Writes sentences that infer something that must have happened between illustrations	66-69	
TIME, RATE AND DISTANCE			**CORRELATED EVENTS**		
Relates the "speed" of a character to the "time" it takes the character to reach a point	42-43		Uses information about correlated events to rank different locations	66	
Answers questions about the amount of time and the speed of characters in a race	44		Completes sentences that refer to correlated events	67	
Uses information about feet per second and answers questions about the amount of time and speed of characters	45-49		**STORY GRAMMAR** **Model Stories** Answers comprehension questions about a story	1-69	
Applies rules about characters' rates to a map that shows a race	51-64		Listens to a familiar story	7-60	
Applies rules about characters' rates in inches per second to a map	53		**Application** Makes a picture consistent with the details of a story	1-69	
Applies rules about characters' rates to a map that shows one character with a head start	54-62		Draws a picture based on a familiar story	14	
Figures out how far racers will be on a course after 1 hour	63		**Extrapolation** Predicts the outcome of a story	23-55	
Discriminates between statements about how far a character goes and how fast the character goes	66-69		Cooperatively composes an episode involving familiar story grammar	27-58	
Uses information about times to formulate rules about characters' rates	66-69		Presents a cooperatively-developed episode based on familiar story grammar	28-59	
			Puts on a play to show part of a familiar story	47-54	
			Plans post-program extension activities	70	

Copyright © by SRA/McGraw-Hill. Permission is granted to reproduce this page for classroom use.

Reproducible Group Summary Sheet — *SUMMARY OF ERRORS*

Names	Test 1			Test 1 Total	Test 2			Test 2 Total	Test 3			Test 3 Total	Test 4			Test 4 Total	Test 5			Test 5 Total	Test 6			Test 6 Total	Test 7			Test 7 Total
	A	B	C		A	B			A	B			A	B	C		A	B			A	B	C		A	B	C	

100 Reasoning and Writing, Level B Guide

Copyright © by SRA/McGraw-Hill. Permission is granted to reproduce this page for classroom use.